THE **PSYCHOLOGY** OF
MARKETING

How Marketers Trick Us Into *Buying More*

HARINDER SINGH PELIA

To all the marketers who, over the years,
convinced me to buy things I never
needed - well played.

You got me.

This book is dedicated to you.

And, of course, screw you.

CONTENTS

1.

INTRODUCTION

*Will This Book Change You
as a Marketer?*

As much as I would like to pretend, I didn't storm out of B-school knowing all the things about marketing and psychology that I do now (or at least I think I do). I walked into a brand management role at an air-conditioning brand - wide-eyed, over-eager and with an alarming sense of confidence that was innocently out of sync with my actual skills as a marketer. I thought that I could come in with "the answer" and change the fortunes of this brand eventually. In my first week, I visualized myself staying there for a while and rising rapidly to become their youngest-ever CMO. I switched in less than 18 months.

Over the years, I hopped across many industries - appliances to smartphones to luxury retail to eCommerce. Sure, there were awards, promotions and wins to fuel my enthusiasm along the way, but there were *many, many, many* more moments when I pitched an idea for a campaign, and got met with blank stares and often polite nods of pity. If I am truly honest, the one thing I lucked out on, was the breadth of consumer segments that I got to work on. One moment, I was working on budget smartphones at Micromax, and the next, I was trying to get rich people to buy ₹30,000 denims at DIESEL. For some months, I even found myself double hatting on SatyaPaul, trying to revive a brand that had yet to rediscover its relevance for the consumer of tomorrow. And just when I thought I was getting the hang of the brands I was juggling, I shifted gears to help build Ajio Luxe, what is now India's foremost luxury eCommerce platform. Next? I had to unlearn everything that I had learned about luxury when Amazon pulled me back into the world of mass-market fashion - a place where scale trumps style.

Through all this, I began to see a pattern. At the fundamental level, it's all the same.

You can complicate things by piling on layers upon layers of consumer, category or industry nuances. However, at the very *core*, triggering attitudinal and behavioral change through marketing follows the same fundamental principles. Maybe we marketers just love complicating things. Sometimes, perhaps, we want to feel worthy of our paychecks, and other times, maybe it's just to protect our turf. We love our models, prisms and ladders that look & sound fancy, but deep down, EACH ONE of those frameworks is built upon a handful of psychological principles that govern our brains. And this book is an attempt to unwrap some of those.

I truly believe that once you understand the *basics of human behavior* and why we do the things that we do - you won't need complex formats or a hundred acronyms in your head. You just need to understand what makes people tick. Once you understand that - mediums, channels, ad formats, creatives, copy, trends, algorithms - everything else becomes secondary.

Understanding the craft of marketing is about deeply understanding *people*. Along the way, the two somehow become inseparable, like tea and biscuits.

Because you're often not selling products, you're selling *feelings*. Marketing is essentially a psychological game - a carefully choreographed dance of motivations, desires, anxiety and often denial. And since you've picked this book up, you've decided to join me on this mildly obsessive journey of unwrapping how marketers get us to buy more through clever psychological tricks. I promise it'll be worth it - if you get to the end and start experimenting with the ideas you find here.

Do We Buy Things, or Do We Buy into Stories?

Do you buy Nike sneakers, or do you buy into the idea of a fitter, more confident *you*? When you buy a FabIndia *kurta*, are you buying just the *kurta*, or are you buying into their tales of craftsmanship, authenticity and ethical sourcing? That's the heart of the debate.

Imagine yourself at D-Mart, trying to buy mango pickle, when suddenly you spot a new brand whose packaging has a smiling grandmother on it. Why is that feeling of nostalgia, warmth and comfort of *Nani ka achar* so irresistible? Why do we pay a hefty premium for Blue Tokai coffee - is it because we don't want to be seen as mainstream, non-connoisseurs who go to Starbucks? Or can we *actually* tell the difference between the coffee? That's the secret sauce: we buy brands based on emotion and then justify our decisions with logic.

There is a lot to discuss, so let's walk through the rabbit holes we'll be diving into, in this book.

The Voices Inside Your Head: Cognitive Biases

Think of *cognitive biases* as the tiny puppeteers that live inside your head, silently nudging your decisions, without you noticing. Good marketers have mastered the art of exploiting these to make you think that you're making a rational decision, even when you're not.

Take the *anchoring effect*. If you see a "Was ₹300, now ₹99" board at a supermarket, chances are you'll pick it up. It's the anchor of ₹300 that's making ₹99 seem like a steal, even if it actually may be worth ₹75 only. We're just buying micro-dopamine hits, aren't we? Or take the *scarcity bias*, the anxiety that hits when you finally like a dress and it says "1 item left", and you hit "Buy Now" with the speed of light. Or *confirmation bias*, when we've decided something and go from pillar to post trying to find data, opinions or reviews to confirm and support what we've already decided in our heads. We'll uncover a bunch of these biases that govern our decision-making.

Why Does ₹9,990 Look Cheaper Than ₹10,000?

Bata has been doing this for ages, and *charm pricing* is the oldest trick in the book. This has nothing to do with logic; it's only an illusion of value and how we read and register digits. Flash sales and lightning deals make us feel compelled not to miss out on the action. There are brands out there making people think they're cheaper than what they are, which works

- but sometimes the reverse works (luxury goods). There's a reason the tall, venti and grande are priced in a certain way at Starbucks - so that you always go for the Grande, and the others act as *decoys*. Or, why does swiping your card for ₹5,000 feel easier than handing over a wad of ₹5,000 in cash to someone? Those are the questions we'll answer in pricing.

Who's the Second Fiddle? Emotion or Logic?

Did you buy your Apple Watch because you wanted to track your steps? Or did you want to project the image of a person in the Apple cult who smashes their workouts every morning and is so busy that they need notifications on their wrist? Our minds play wonderful tricks, and brands like Apple know how to weaponise them against us.

One may argue that most decisions are *90% emotion and 10% logic*, even if we don't want to acknowledge it as such. Marketers know that logic matters, but often, it's only *after* the buying decision is already made in the customer's head. You use the crutches of logic to *justify* the decision that emotions have already made for you. You love the camera capabilities of the new Samsung Galaxy, but you can't help buying another iPhone. The excuse you'll outwardly give is that "I am too used to the interface; it's too easy", when the emotional reason is that you don't want to be the only person in your social circle with an Android in your hand. It's wonderful irrationality at its finest.

The Art of Making the Customer Say Yes, Through Persuasion

Here, we'll go over Robert Cialdini's work, which is as effective for making someone buy shampoo as it is for making someone go out on a date with you. The principles of *persuasion and pre-suasion* have stood the test of time and are as potent in the digital age as they were in the TV era.

If you've seen people outside the mall offering you a rose or an Indian flag pin and then quickly soliciting a donation out of you - that's the principle of *reciprocity*. Then there's *social proof, liking, scarcity* and a lot else. Dr. Cialdini's work is my personal favorite due to its deceptive simplicity and applicability.

The New Currency in the Age of Instagram Reels: Your Attention

We've all been hearing that data is the new oil, but arguably it's attention. Every brand wants a piece of yours, and every platform wants to harvest and sell it to the top bidder. Marketers will do just about anything to grab hold of your attention: colors, sounds, countdown timers, notifications - anything!

We'll go through some scholarly work (*not boring, promise*) on how our brain filters out the unnecessary and decides what to pay attention to and for how long. This is followed by ways to hack attention in the short term through visual, auditory and other cues. And wherever there are tricks to hack attention, they should also be supplemented with a debate on whether any of it is ethical at all, and what needs to be done about it.

What Drives Every Click and Swipe: Motivation

Motivation is the most misunderstood word in our world. What drives us *intrinsically*, and what drives us *extrinsically*? How do marketers know when to trigger what, to make us feel like it was our idea? The pull of an external reward or discount is very different from the voice that intrinsically comes from within us to buy into a brand, join a club or become a loyalist.

In the motivation section, we whip out five theories that should make you sound smarter at dinner parties (*I use them a lot!*). This demystifies the interplay of intention, control and where we think we are in our personal and social lives. We'll also talk about something that we fall for every day: impulse buying and how that Dairy Milk at the checkout counter magically makes its way into our supermarket carts.

The Illusion of Choice

The myth of having a choice is perhaps capitalism's favorite trick. We're fed to believe that more options mean more choice & freedom, when more choices just overwhelm us and ensure that we stick to familiar, default choices. Some of us are *maximizers* who evaluate every feature, detail and review, and some of us are *satisficers* for whom "good enough" is enough.

Real decision-making isn't as logical and straightforward as the *Rational Choice Theory* suggests - it's messy and often bounded with time and information, as *Bounded Rationality* concepts tell us. Marketers all around us shape our choices day and night with nudges, pre-selected options and clever store layouts. This chapter will make you agree that we're way more manipulated than what we admit.

Why You Keep Coming Back for More: Habits & Loyalty

The ultimate aim for most brands would be to turn themselves into habits. Using *habit loops* (*cue, routine, reward*), brands like Cult.fit have made fitness more than a chore - it feels like a community-driven addiction for the platform's power users.

True *brand loyalty*, however, is super rare. Most marketers mistake frequent and heavy buying for loyalty, which is far from the truth. True loyalty builds an emotional connection that even cheaper and better competitors find tough to break. The *loyalty ladder* suggests how we can nudge customers to go from awareness to advocacy, but we can never push them forward. In the end, you can lure the customer into a habit, but the way to their heart - that's a privilege that only true loyalty can earn.

Does AI (or an MRI Machine) Know You Better Than Your Mom?

AI has gone from sci-fi movies to becoming a marketer's new best (or worst) friend. We can seamlessly get AI to do our dirty work and make it predict what our customers would want, even before they know it. But we still get creeped out when we talk about going to Japan with our friends, and somehow, our Instagram feed suddenly becomes plastered with Japanese travel content. AI's got to remain a helpful sidekick and not try to become a creepy stalker who often tries to act human.

Neuromarketing is another shiny tool in the modern marketer's arsenal. What consumers *think, say, feel and do* - are often four different things, and neuromarketing helps get real answers, even if it means putting customers under an fMRI machine to see how their brains light up to things we put in front of their eyes. Focus groups are still inefficient, with people wanting to look good in front of others while hiding their true opinions. Neuromarketing is super effective but also raises questions around ethics and manipulation.

What Lies Ahead?

We're not only customers; we're part of a giant, sophisticated psychological experiment. Clever marketers use psychology to sell *meaning, identity and stories* that touch us at a deep, emotional level. The intention of writing this book was not only to enable everyone to spot those tricks, but also to help them use these tricks to their advantage.

I think that any marketer, founder, advertising professional, content creator, film-maker… anyone can grasp these psychological tricks and become a true *chameleon*. You'll be able to thrive in any medium:

digital, physical or whatever bizarre thing is called the metaverse (even if your life's aim is to get people to use digital money to buy pixelated jpegs of chimps, called NFTs). Because behind every channel, algorithm, and creative execution - you'll find the same primal triggers of human emotions.

It doesn't matter if you're shooting a hook scene for a 30-second Instagram Reel, or if you're designing a full-page ad for the Times of India or if you're placing your hand cream at eye level in a Reliance Fresh aisle - the psychology of marketing doesn't change. The recipe remains very familiar - FOMO, urgency, social proof, motivation, attention, etc.

The half-life of marketing knowledge is getting shorter every passing year. What you know today, is likely to become outdated in a few years (if not already). So, a deep understanding of *the fundamentals behind the fundamentals of marketing* will make you golden - no matter where marketing goes next.

2.

LEARNING

Are We Trainable Lab Rats?

DIESEL has always been synonymous with those effortlessly cool jackets - the kind that would make you feel like James Dean (or Ranbir Kapoor in his *Animal* entry scene), ready to ride your Harley-Davidson into the sunset without a care in the world.

Let me tell you about the time that I made up my mind to buy a leather jacket - a jacket that was supposed to change my life (or at least my wardrobe). You know that leather jacket. The one that makes you feel like a God, wind in your hair, no smile - because really cool guys *never* smile. And there it was: the perfect leather jacket. Dark, very leathery and with just the right amount of rebellion to suggest that the wearer might be the kind of person who would say random, mysterious things like "I don't make plans." I swiped my credit card faster than my spouse could call me out on my premature mid-life crisis.

I took it back home, slipped it on and looked at myself in the mirror, and it felt… fine. Just fine. There was no sudden surge of machismo, no cinematic wind in my hair. But I quickly put on the cloak of denial. Instead of taking it back to the store, I convinced myself that the leather jacket was an *essential*. Maybe it wasn't about an immediate transformation - maybe I had not worn it in the right light yet.

What's the trick behind this rationalization that I eventually ended up doing? For a leather jacket that makes me look like a circus monkey? (*Note: readers are encouraged to write to the author for pictorial proof of this*).

When I walked into that DIESEL store and laid eyes upon that leather jacket, I wasn't just buying a jacket; I was buying into years of learned behavior, responses that had been conditioned with cleverly delivered psychological nudges. Over the years, I had perhaps learned and built up this image of what it meant to be a free-spirited, devil-may-care kind of guy who wears his leather jacket on his custom Harley. Pavlovian associations, reward systems, cognitive dissonance - all of these things worked silently over the years to create that blurry image in my mind. And that's when it hit me - marketing was less about *what* you buy and more about *what you've been trained to* buy.

In this chapter, we'll talk about how we're learning and observing machines, and all this adds up when we're at the point of making a decision on what and why to buy. Let's see the game for what it actually is.

Pavlov, Rats and Habits

We've all read about conditioning, not the kind you get from running a half-marathon (which you probably signed up for after seeing a promoted post of). But I am talking about the far more psychological kind - *classical and operant* conditioning, the learning tools that have been shaping us since we were mere toddlers.

First, let's talk about classical conditioning: you've heard the story about Pavlov and his salivating dogs.

In his famous experiment, Pavlov rings a bell, the dog gets food and after enough repetitions, the dog starts drooling at the sound of the bell alone. Now, swap dogs for humans and food for the sound of your phone's push notifications. And there you go - you've drooled your way into buying yet another pair of shoes from Myntra.

Have you ever seen an ad for a luxury brand's fragrances? It's always a weird montage showing an extravagant lifestyle. A bottle of perfume isn't projected to be just a mere bottle of perfume. It's shown as the hero in a monochrome film, at a Parisian cafe, with an impossibly chic person with cheekbones that they could slit their own wrists with. Every time you see an ad like that, the association between that brand and high fashion/lifestyle keeps getting stronger and stronger until one fine day, you buy the same perfume, and you expect the same Parisian air to waft through your mundane life. Well, it doesn't.

Now, onto operant conditioning. B.F. Skinner trained rats to pull a lever for food as a reward through the power of positive reinforcement. The same applies to your Third Wave Coffee app. Every coffee gets you tantalizingly close to a free coffee, but not *too* close, because then you'll stop chasing it.

Think about the time when you saw a "Buy 4, get 5th FREE" deal at D-Mart. You didn't even want 5 Epigamia Greek yogurts, but by the time you picked up yogurt #3, more yogurts almost felt like an investment. That's the genius of operant conditioning: small incremental rewards strategically positioned to make you feel like you've got an amazing deal when you've just spent Rs. 1000 on dairy-based desserts, which you really didn't need.

Like an innocent lab rat, we've been trained to respond to associations and reward stimuli. The bell rings, and we start salivating. The reward dangles in front of us like a carrot, and we can't stop our hands from going towards our wallets. All this, while marketers sit back and congratulate themselves for convincing you that your next purchase will finally create that lifestyle upgrade that you've been chasing since the last purchase.

We don't like admitting that we get played, but we do.

Do Influencers Quietly Run Our Lives?

Be super honest with me for one second. Did you buy that gut cleanse detox kit because you *really* needed it? Or did you buy it on the nudge of that influencer on your feed who, bathed in soft lighting, was chugging it down like it was some secret to inner purity? You chanced upon her paid post and followed her perfectly curated online life, and suddenly, you're on the GoodBug website, convinced that it's the missing ingredient for your perfect future life.

This is what Albert Bandura called *observational learning* in his well-cited *Social Learning Theory*. He articulated this in 1977, much before today's world of influencers. We're not just learning *what* to buy from these modern-day gurus, but we're somehow learning how to *live*. And in today's day and age, there's nobody better than influencers to subtly get you to try new products by projecting that they've got life all figured out.

We all love Virat Kohli. But when he spoke about his plant-based diet, suddenly half of Instagram was talking about replacing their butter chicken with pea protein shakes. Vegetarian uncles had a field day on WhatsApp, sending forwards about the wonders of vegetarianism. It's not about the protein powder he's using - what matters is that HE is using it. So when Kohli comes and says, "I used <random> protein powder", you're not buying into the product only. You're buying a piece of his disciplined, high-standards aura.

That's *consumer socialization* in its modern 2020s, social-media-approved form. Influencers aren't just peddling products - they're selling aspiration. And the genius of it all is that it often doesn't seem like marketing - it seems like advice.

Influencers (at least the good ones) don't shout out, "Hey You! Buy this Shit!"; they subtly suggest that you should check it out, and it just might be what you were looking for. You're not actively buying - you're learning to be a better/cooler/healthier version of yourself. And that's why even though you barely drink enough coffee, you somehow end up owning a hipster drip-coffee apparatus. And you think that this, finally, will cement your position in your social circle as a budding coffee connoisseur.

How Brands Successfully Hijack Our Brain's Filing System

Our brain has this strangely chaotic yet beautiful filing system. We constantly try to make sense of the endless stream of information, stimuli and a whole lot of ads that get thrown at us. And if there's one thing that the best marketers are really good at, it's making sure that their brand gets prime real estate in our brain's mental filing cabinet. Somehow.

If you have to understand the *information processing theory* - you must think of our brain as this overworked corporate employee who's always running out of breath trying to classify, store, encode, and retrieve information by using as little energy as possible. And that's where the marketer's job comes in - we're the ones slipping small post-it notes onto your desk with ads and shiny logos that you can't somehow seem to forget (even if you tried to).

Think of it like one big game of Tetris. Brands are those little blocks which fall one after the other, trying to lock themselves into place so that the next time you're looking to make a decision - say to buy a toothpaste - the name Colgate pops up faster than someone else can say '*dentists dwara pramaanit*'.

We all have a bottle of Eno in our homes. Every time there's even a slight hint of indigestion (after wolfing down that plate of *chole bhature*), the first thing that comes to mind is, "*Eno, kaam shuru sirf 6 second mein.*" This is because Eno has brilliantly embedded itself into your brain's protocol for acidity or gassy episodes. Their clever ads have cemented the connection between over-indulgent eating and instant relief (with a grand burp). The imagery of Eno's fizzing action is well entrenched in our collective memories.

Eno's not just selling a solution; they stand for assured results (*that satisfying burp*). You start thinking that whenever your stomach rebels, then Eno will be your first line of defense. And this is not because you've researched the science behind antacids - it's because that familiar green-and-white packaging and that bubbling action now stands for a mental shortcut that says 'problem solved'. That's Information Processing 101, that Eno is so neatly filed away in your mind's digestive distress folder that considering anything else would just seem illogical.

Marketers use this to their advantage. They know that you're not always making decisions based on careful, rational analysis. You're just retrieving information from pre-stored and filed data in your brain. Hence, they sneak into that filing cabinet through repetitive ads that are catchy and packed with emotional triggers.

Who else craves Maggi when they're burning the midnight oil? That bright yellow packet is not just a familiar pack of instant noodles; it's a part of our childhood memories. The aroma of Maggi being made in 2-minutes (well, 10 if we're being truly honest) - that fragrance is carefully tucked away in your mental filing cabinet so that the next time you're craving comfort food, you reach out for Maggi without even thinking twice.

So, the human brain is a battleground, after all. Brands are trying to dislodge each other for a spot on your filing system. Because they know that once they're in, then it's quite hard to get them out. You may think that you're actively making decisions, but more often than not, you're just retrieving the most conveniently placed information from your mental archives. It's not only about choice; it's also about recall.

Your Brain's a Walking Billboard

You're standing in a supermarket and there are 30 different biscuit brands in the aisles in front of you. And yet, without a second thought, your hand instinctively picks up a packet of Parle-G. Why? Is it because you carefully evaluated the ingredients and nutritional content? Or did you look out for reviews on its greater *dunkability*? No, you didn't. It's because your brain already has Parle-G filed under "comfort biscuits", and you pulled the file before you realized you did.

Consumer memory and recall are critical parts of the consumer's brain. Our brain, like a dusty archive, works to retrieve brand associations that it filed years ago. As we discussed earlier, this seldom works on logic alone but on repetition and emotion. Parle-G didn't become the best-selling biscuit brand in India by accident. It was gradually encoded into our childhood memories and reinforced with images of evening chai and sutta at the *tapri* with colleagues. It's not a mere biscuit - it's a memory trigger.

Now, let's talk about Vicks. The unique smell of Vicks VapoRub reminds you of cold winter evenings when your mother's gentle hand rubbed it onto your chest and the relief that followed soon after. Vicks reminds you not only of cough relief but also of the experience of being cared for and feeling safe with your mother. So, when you're down with a cold as an adult, what does your brain tell you? "I need that smell, that familiar smell" as a memory of comfort.

In the endless battle for consumer loyalty, the winners are often NOT the brands with the best products, but those which have quietly and surely stored themselves in the far reaches of your brain for years, silently waiting for the moment when you need them the most. And in that moment, you're not exactly making an active choice; you're recalling a core memory.

The Psychology of Reinforcement Schedules

If we're truly honest with ourselves, the promise of a good deal keeps us going back to certain brands. It's a well-played psychological game where the key is to give out rewards that keep coming but not always when the customer expects them to.

We love (and hate) scratch cards that Google Pay gives us as cashback. Every time you pay with Google Pay, they give you a tantalizing chance of winning a cashback, but it is never guaranteed. More often than not, you would end up getting that infuriating '*Better Luck Next Time.*' But sometimes you get ₹3 back, and once in a blue moon, even ₹30. That's the genius of the *variable-ratio reinforcement schedule*. It's like playing the slot machine at a casino. Every payment made you curious to scratch the card, and every small win kept you coming back more in search of a big cashback.

We remember *Big Bazaar's Wednesday Bazaar* when they used to have crazy discounts on groceries and staples on the same day every week. This is a classic example of *interval reinforcement*. The timing is fixed - you know what to expect from Big Bazaar every Wednesday, and the offers are just good enough to make you come back next week.

Even Reliance Trends uses reinforcement schedules well. You walk into their stores and see promotions like "Spend ₹5,000 and get a voucher of ₹1,000 for your next purchase." This is what is called *fixed-ratio reinforcement* - you know exactly what the reward is, and you also know when and how you'll get it. You've already spent ₹4,000, and you feel drawn to spend just a little bit more to hit that ₹5,000 mark. Once you get that voucher, you obviously have a compelling reason to return to shop again. So it's a clever cycle: they get you to shop a bit more and also return again - all while thinking that you got a solid deal.

Reinforcement schedules try to turn your spending into a repetitive habit in some way - whether it's paying via UPI, looking for grocery deals or spending more on clothes. The rewards are smartly spaced out to keep you on the hook, and unknowingly, you're trained to come back for that next hit of dopamine.

Why You Bought That Overpriced Air Purifier: The Elaboration Likelihood Model

I grew up in Delhi, so I am more touchy than average on the topic of air quality. We've all bought air purifiers at some point or wanted to buy them.

Let me take you to the day I bought one. You know, the one that costs almost as much as a smartphone but now sits quietly in a corner, humming away like an expensive reminder of your brief flirtation with the idea of "breathing in healthy air at all times." While I bought it, something called the *Elaboration Likelihood Model* (ELM) was at play.

ELM (Petty and Cacioppo, 1980) shows two routes to persuasion: *central and peripheral.* Think of *Central Processing* as your inner nerd who kicks in whenever you find something that you really care about and want to research to the last detail. You're looking at specifications and reviews and asking people questions over WhatsApp. And *Peripheral Processing* is pretty much your brain being on autopilot - getting swayed by ads, offers and shiny ads and saying, "Ya, this looks cool."

Getting back to the air purifier, I walked into the store, well aware that pollution levels were at an all-time high, so *central processing* was fully in action. I started looking at filtration levels, deciding between HEPA or activated carbon filters. The air purifier is not only a gadget now; it's an investment in my family's lungs and overall health.

But that's the story we want to tell ourselves. It's far from being the complete truth. The *peripheral route* is also at play here. I guess I saw an ad some time back with a celeb recommending the same air purifier. Or my eye caught the claim on the packaging that says "*India's Most Trusted Air Purifier Brand.*" Maybe the design caught my eye; it would surely look great sitting in one corner of my living room. Suddenly, those hours of research didn't matter as much as this did. The brand FELT trustworthy, the celebrity is someone I trust, and the claims seem legit. There! I was sold. Swipe, Pack, Done.

ELM is a great way to gauge how customers are evaluating your products. People are very invested in some products and less in others. Brands need to make sure they load these customers up with specs and comparison charts - to target *central processing*. But they must also sprinkle some *peripheral triggers* to make them feel confident in their purchase without having to do a PhD in air filtration. This way, whether you encounter a detail freak or someone for whom a good ad is enough, you'll have both covered.

Your Ignored Smartwatch and the Power of Cognitive Dissonance

Last Prime Day, I finally gave in and bought an Apple Watch. I had always been suspicious of smartwatches, but I got a crazy deal, and this purchase was supposed to revolutionize my life. The Apple Watch was meant to make me healthier, more productive, and, if their ads are to be believed, a *better* version of myself. I was mighty convinced that this tiny wrist computer was going to track my steps, organize my life, help me sleep better, and maybe get me that six-pack one day. I hit "Buy Now" and eagerly awaited the delivery.

The watch arrived, and you've got to give it to Apple for making packaging that's just impossible to throw away. The watch was shiny, futuristic, and seemed like having a personal assistant on my wrist. But after a few days of using it, a strange feeling crept in. I realized that I wasn't as happy with it as I thought I would be. The fitness goals? Ignored. Sleep? Not tracked. The notifications? Annoying beyond a point. But did I return it? Nope. That's *cognitive dissonance*.

When you make a big purchase like this one, we expect it to deliver on the promises that we've made up in our heads. But when reality doesn't meet this fantasy, then our brains play a clever little trick - they work overtime to justify the purchase rather than admitting that we had made a mistake buying it. Why does this happen? Because we humans *hate* being wrong. The discomfort of accepting that we've wasted money is so unpleasant that we use weird logic to avoid facing it.

After a week of minimal use of my Apple Watch, I caught myself saying things like "I love the ECG feature" and "I will close my fitness goal rings starting next week" - anything to convince myself that it remained a good purchase.

That's the beauty of cognitive dissonance for marketers like us. It creates a strange kind of *loyalty*. One has to do all kinds of mental gymnastics to ensure that you feel your purchase is worth it and that you're invested in the brand. Returning the product would be a personal defeat. The behavior shifts - not because the product is revolutionary, but because I have convinced myself that it is.

Cognitive dissonance explains why people stick to brands even when they fall short of competition. Your smartphone lags too much? It's still "a cult" or "I could never use an Android, eww." That expensive pair of Jordans that pinch a little? "They just need to be broken in a bit." We rationalize the choice we've made so much that we forget that we're doing it because we're convinced that we made the right choice all along.

The Sneaky Role of Cultural Influences

We know by now that we don't just buy products; we buy into *stories*. And stories are often deep-rooted in culture. These cultural narratives are far more influential than the specs of the new iPhone or the quality of the fabric of the Hugo Boss polo t-shirt that you've been eyeing for a while. Culture is the silent force that nudges our decisions at an individual as well as family level.

Let's talk about one of the most hated brands of recent times, Fair & Lovely (now *Glow and Lovely* to be politically correct). Now, I'm not here to debate the ethics of selling fairness creams - though there's plenty to say about that - the point we need to make is that people don't buy the tube because it has great moisturizing properties. They buy it because, unfortunately, *generations* of cultural conditioning in India tell us that fairer skin equates to beauty, confidence and even career success. Indian society has reinforced this association through decades of learning through films, ads (even matrimonial ones) and brands like Fair and Lovely take advantage of that deep-rooted (yet, misplaced) cultural nuance.

That's the role of culture. It doesn't exactly tell you *what* to buy, but it shapes your thinking about *why* you need it in the first place.

We've all had Bournvita while growing up. Here again, you're not buying a chocolate-flavored powder to mix in milk; you're buying into the idea of strong, tall, healthy children - an idea being peddled since the 90s. We, Indians, put massive emphasis on education and physical growth of our children. So much so that their academic performance and height can sometimes feel like a reflection of the kind of parenting they've received. Bournvita plays to these cultural expectations and becomes your child's "*tayyari jeet ki*" in this hyper-competitive, modern world.

Or take Kalyan Jewellers - a brand that aims to represent Indian culture, draped in gold. They want you to think that you're not buying jewelry - but you're buying into the essence of tradition. Their imagery shows traditions around gold and the pride of passing on gold heirlooms to the next generation. I think they've mastered the art of using our cultural obsession with gold, heritage and weddings against us. Their communication talks about something larger culturally - family and tradition, and tries to connect to our cultural identities as Indians.

Culture also often dictates how brands have to adapt to regional differences. Enough has been said about McDonald's doing a McAloo Tikki burger to win in India, so we won't delve into that. However, what we need to grasp is how beautifully cultural influences affect consumer learning in such a subtle and silent way. Brands that tap into culture focus less on promoting products and more on aligning values, aspirations and narratives. Because brands know that once they harness the power of culture, they stop being a choice and start becoming an extension of who we are.

TURN INSIGHTS INTO ACTION

→ Classical and Operant Conditioning

- ◆ Pair your products with positive stimuli (like families in ads, upbeat music, and aspirational lifestyle) to trigger positive emotions when people think about your brand

- ◆ Create reward systems using operant conditioning that encourage loyalty and repeat purchases through their search for dopamine

→ Social Learning Theory

- ◆ Leverage high-trust influencers that your target audience would like to mimic

- ◆ Influencers should use the product in aspirational yet relatable contexts

- ◆ Don't shy away from user-generated content and micro-influencers; they add credibility

→ Information Processing Theory

- ◆ Make messaging clear, transparent and repeatable. Earworm jingles help.

- ◆ Hooks are the most essential part of any ad, make them stand out in the initial encoding process

- ◆ Break down information into fileable chunks (e.g. 3 benefits of this air purifier)

→ Reinforcement Schedules

- Tie your brand to positive emotional experiences from everyday life

- Leverage nostalgia to trigger consumers' fond memories, so that they are emotionally invested in your brand

→ Elaboration Likelihood Model (ELM)

- Appeal to both detailed and cursory thinkers in your communication

- Balance emotional and rational appeal, never over-index on either

→ Cognitive Dissonance

- Reinforce satisfaction post-purchase by follow-ups and feedback surveys

- Highlight peer validation to make the consumer feel like the 'odd one out' if they dislike the product

→ Cultural Influences

- Try and link your brand to the cultural identity of your target audience, thus reinforcing bonds beyond the product alone

3.

MOTIVATION

That Misunderstood Word.

Motivation is one of those terms that get thrown around far too much and are understood far too little. It's that invisible voice that gets you out of bed - or keeps you glued to it (depending on how comfortable your duvet is). It's the voice in your head that makes you click "add to cart" at midnight for something that you will surely never need, but in the moment you think you can't live without. It's a game that can be learned and used to win.

We've all seen those air fryer ads on Instagram, dreaming of making guilt-free *pakoras*, only to see it now sitting in one corner of the kitchen, alone and staring at you. Ever wondered how Starbucks makes you spend ₹400 on a cappuccino that experts consider average at best? It's because these folks have cracked the motivation code. They understand how to stir up your innermost desires - whether it's for social acceptance or the need to project a certain image through smug eco-friendly, upcycled fashion (*ya, nobody cares about that*).

Let's go on a journey through the murky waters of motivation, by the end of which we'll probably acknowledge that we're puppets at best, being skillfully nudged by our innermost desires.

Intrinsic Motivation: Strikes from Within

Picture this: it's a fine Sunday morning, and you're sipping an overpriced, yet weirdly bitter, cold brew at your favorite cafe. You're feeling cool and experiencing an inflated sense of importance and indulgence. You love the cafe's vibe and feel that "I'm a regular here" even though you've been coming here for just two weeks. Then it suddenly hits you - the itch. The itch to do something meaningful.

So what do you do? You whip out your phone and start scrolling Reels. And you stumble on a hobby that you'll abandon in less than a week. Yoga? Oh yes, perfect. The mindfulness, the flexibility, the wellness… and the trendy yoga mats on Amazon. You buy a yoga mat, a new pair of yoga pants and a water bottle even before you finish your coffee.

That's *intrinsic motivation*. You didn't buy these things because someone showed you a discount. You bought them because you felt that they'll genuinely help you achieve your new yogi/yogini state of self. This is what marketers drool at - when people want to buy things because of reasons that feel personal and authentic. It's the kind of motivation that gets people to sign up for marathons and, god forbid, start podcasts (*the author is guilty as charged on this count*).

Brands and marketers know that when intrinsic motivation strikes, you're not just buying for rewards; you're buying to build the idea of the person you think you are or want to become.

Extrinsic motivation - the shiny carrot

Now, let's jump onto the other kind of motivation. You're minding your own business at the mall when suddenly a sign that reads "*All-you-can-eat Pizza for*

Rs. 599" grabs you by the gut and collar. You weren't planning on doing a food challenge today. In fact, you had come to the mall to return those ill-fitting jeans that you bought last week. But somehow, here you are, walking out of the restaurant after having eaten an ungodly number of pizzas and having unbuttoned your jeans.

Well, this is *extrinsic motivation*. This is where discounts, offers, rewards, etc., pressure you to buy. It's like the classic carrot and stick approach that has been driving human behavior since time immemorial. You're buying it because you're getting an insane deal, and you're not foolish to miss out on those, right?

Loyalty programs (if done right) are a marketer's dream. You walk into Third Wave Coffee, and you leave with loyalty points that whisper in your ear, "You're a step closer to a free coffee!" It doesn't matter that you'll need to buy three more overpriced cappuccinos before you can actually get your free one. This is gamified caffeine consumption at its best, driven by a healthy dose of extrinsic motivation.

Extrinsic motivation is predictable, powerful and also vanishes quickly. Sure, you got a Flat 50% at Lacoste this time, but what happens when there isn't? You move on; the motivation disappears, much like the brown sugar in your overpriced cappuccino. Your motivation for walking into Lacoste was predicated on the deal that was dangled in front of you. The challenge for marketers is not just dangling the carrot but also to keep you interested once it's gone.

Every Marketer's Favorite Pyramid Scheme: Maslow

If there's one thing that psychologists love more than Venn diagrams, it's a pyramid. Maslow's Hierarchy of Needs Pyramid (1943) is kind of like the Swiss army knife of marketing. What started as an innocent theory about human motivation has become a blueprint for modern marketers to make you buy things that you didn't know existed, let alone that you needed.

At the base of the pyramid, you have all your *physiological* needs: *roti, kapda, and makaan.* Sounds simple, right? Nope. Take bottled water, for example. What could be more basic than this? And yet, somehow marketers have turned purified water into a premium wellness drink by slapping words like "glacier-sourced", "alkaline" on the label. And somehow, you're paying ₹50 for a 500 ml. bottle of RO water because now it comes with a side dish of moral & socioeconomic superiority.

Then there's the insurance industry, playing at the *'safety'* level of the pyramid. They're not selling policies, but they're selling peace of mind wrapped in paranoia. When you buy health insurance, you're buying into the assurance that if you spontaneously combust tomorrow, your family will still be able to afford dinner. Insurance brands are in the business of selling the "What if?" And let's face it, who doesn't like their monthly insurance premiums to come sprinkled with a seasoning of existential dread?

Move up the Maslow ladder, and we get to the part about *connection.* Of course, we have to talk about Apple here. When you buy an iPhone, you don't just buy a device to watch more Instagram Reels on; you're buying your way into a club. It's a shiny, curated membership that says, "I am rich and love tech & design." Why else would people queue up for hours to get their hands on the new iPhone like they're auditioning for *Roadies*?

Then, we hit the *esteem* level. Luxury brands do this better than most. They tap into our need to be noticed and show people that we've arrived in life. It's why a Louis Vuitton bag isn't only a bag - it's a walking billboard that reads, "I've made it in life!" When I was heading marketing for DIESEL, we knew that we weren't only selling expensive jeans; we were selling the idea that slipping into a new pair of DIESELs made you instantly cooler, more desirable and more rebellious. At least in your head. A Patek Philippe isn't just a watch; it's a declaration of status. Like they say, "You wear a watch to tell the time. I wear a Patek to tell you how valuable my time is."

Finally, at the top of the pyramid, we find the Holy Grail - the pinnacle of human motivation - *self-actualization*. This is where sustainable brands like *No Nasties* try and play. You're not just buying a shirt; you're making a bold statement about your values, ethics, and deep concern for sustainability and the environment you'll leave behind for future generations. Doesn't matter if the only 'green' thing in your life is the bottle of Aloe Vera gel on your bathroom shelf and the plants you smoked back in college. Buying from

No Nasties isn't about the fabric - it's about expressing yourself through your brand choices and making a moral statement each time you use it.

Motivators You Should Milk: McClelland's Acquired Needs

David McClelland gave marketers a dream roadmap to human motivation in 1961. His Acquired Needs Theory boils down motivation into three categories: *achievement, affiliation and power.*

If you truly get the gist of this, you won't only be able to figure out what drives your close ones, but also find a treasure map to consumers' wallets. Let's unwrap this.

Achievement

Achievement junkies (particularly those on LinkedIn) love it when you give them a goal. Give them a mountain to metaphorically (or actually) climb, and they'll not think twice before going all-in. Great marketers know that it's never actually about the achievement, but it's about the *feeling* of achievement. Nike isn't a mere shoe brand - they're selling the dopamine rush that comes with convincing yourself that today's 20-minute run will one day compound into an ultramarathon triumph.

Fitness apps use this well. Fitbit and Strava are digital peddlers who hand out micro-doses of the achievement drug like a strong espresso. You track every step, every run and every hour of sleep. You become addicted not to the app but to the idea of fitness, tracking progress and unlocking achievements. So, if you come across a heart monitor or smart-scale, to start tracking and achieving more, why not?

Affiliation

Affiliation is every human's need to *belong*. If you've ever been to CULT, you know what I am talking about. It's not just a place to sweat - it's like a temple of community spirit. You don't go to just exercise; you go to *belong* to the cult. If you do a few months of CULT, you're sure to become a part of their tribe of protein powder devotees, grunting away through burpees.

And, of course, you post about it - #WeAreCult with the enthusiasm of a new convert. Cult is hitting at the urban loneliness epidemic and creating a space that is less about lifting weights and more about lifting your social game. Because nothing says that you're one of the gang, like sweating together in an HRX workout, right?

Power

Power is that heady cocktail that gives you this intoxicating feeling of being influential and in control. And looking *very* successful. This is where luxury brands play - with their fancy handbags, watches and overpriced hype sneakers. Tory Burch bags aren't only for carrying things - they are for *carrying yourself* - right to the top of the socioeconomic ladder.

After a decade of slogging at your corporate job, you've earned (*at least that's what you tell yourself*) the right to drop ₹50,000 on a handbag that tells the world that you've made it. The handbag is just a visual ad for your newfound power, without uttering a word. It's subtle and just about as modest as the red supercars parked outside DLF Emporio.

How Marketers Let You Think You're the Boss (Even When You're Not): Self-Determination Theory

Self-Determination Theory (Deci and Ryan, 1985) is a marketer's way of telling you that they're going to let you believe that you're in the driver's seat even when someone is pulling the strings. SDT told us about three basic human needs: *autonomy* (the illusion that you're running the show), *competence* (the feeling of being good at something, even if you're not) and *relatedness* (the glue that holds us all together socially).

Autonomy

Being *free* is fundamentally one of the most important things to a human being. We love to think that we're making our own decisions and building our own lives ourselves. Enter IKEA. You walk through the labyrinth of a showroom and carefully choose a piece of furniture that "perfectly expresses your individuality" - feeling like an aesthetic visionary. But what you don't realize is that IKEA has pre-decided your choices for you. From the time you entered, they showed you the right natural palette colors in a flattering light - so that when you came to the sofa whose name nobody can pronounce, you thought it was your idea to choose this color. So you leave with a cart full of boxes, beaming with pride at the idea of building your furniture yourself. Marketers need to make customers feel like they're fully autonomous and acting without any external influence.

Competence

Imagine the feeling of saying, "I think I'm actually getting the hang of this!" - that's how competence makes apps like Duolingo so addictive. You start with an innocent "Bonjour", and in a few weeks, you start imagining yourself ordering coffee and butter croissants at a Parisian cafe in fluent French. Sure, you'll open your mouth and probably sound like a tourist, but Duolingo makes you "feel" competent. They've gamified it well so that you're more focused on completing your streak than using your French out in the wild. But does that even matter? Duolingo gives you dopamine hits when you hit each level and feel like a genius.

Relatedness

We're herd animals with a deep-seated need to connect. Nothing feels like being a part of a community. Twitch, the live-streaming service, lets gamers watch live streams while also making it a proper conversation. They're not only passively watching someone else play; they're an active part of the experience, chatting with hundreds and thousands of others, sharing their comments, insights and memes. Twitch taps into the need for relatedness in a very organic way. It's like hanging out with your friends and playing Minecraft without actually having to leave the house. They've built a virtual campfire where you can share ghost stories with folks from around the globe.

"Probably I Will, Eventually": The Theory of Planned Behaviour

You make up your mind to hit the gym tomorrow, and when tomorrow arrives, there isn't a force in the world that can separate you from your bed. In its simplest form, the Theory of Planned Behaviour (Ajzen, 1985) says that all our actions are a function of three parameters: *attitudes* (how we feel), *subjective norms* (what we think others expect of us) and *perceived behavioral control* (how easy or hard we think it will be). It's the ultimate "should I vs. shouldn't I" equation.

Attitudes

Marketing is fundamentally about shaping attitudes favorably towards a brand or product. Take electric cars, for example. A decade ago, the idea of driving a glorified golf cart (*I am looking at you Reva*) was about as appealing as getting a tooth extraction without anesthesia. But then Tesla entered with its irresistible aura of being seen as futuristic and forward-thinking. And suddenly, driving an EV was not just for tree-hugging hippies or virgin computer science graduates. In India, Ather, Ola, Tata and Mahindra have slowly turned EVs into a more practical and future-ready choice for buyers. Attitudes have now shifted from "Will I ever drive an EV?" to "When should I get an EV?" and that's a big win.

Subjective Norms

Peer pressure, as we all know now, doesn't stop at school. *Subjective norms* are what we think everyone expects us to do. Why do you think your Instagram Reels feed is full of influencers pushing keto meal services? You didn't actually want to go carb-free, but after seeing those endless gym selfies and 'cheat day' hashtags, you suddenly ask if you're missing the boat. It's FOMO wrapped in a Keto burrito. Brands know that once they make you believe that "everyone's doing it", you're far more likely to jump onto the bandwagon.

Perceived Behavioural Control

Here's where you evaluate how easy or how tough the task will be to pull off. Once upon a time, ordering food was a test of your patience. Find the restaurant's menu in the drawer, call them, explain the order five times and pray that they don't forget your request for extra *chutney*. But then Swiggy and Zomato arrived and made the process magical. Click, swipe and voila! Your biryani is on its way. You even get to track the delivery guy to feed your trust issues - no more *'ladka nikal gaya hai.'*

When your brain doesn't perceive any barrier between *intention and action*, no effort or potential heartburn, your wallet almost opens by itself.

Why You Expect the Best: Expectancy-Value Theory

This fancy-sounding theory basically means this: we do things because we expect something good in return.

Whether it's going to the gym, buying lottery tickets, or buying yet another pair of Jordans, we think this *could be* worth it, finally.

Nowhere is this more apparent than in the eCommerce festive sales that happen every Diwali. Flipkart and Amazon turn into high-stakes *subz-mandis* offering discounts that are so mouth-watering that you feel like a genius for having spotted them in time. Do you really need another pair of noise-canceling headphones? Of course not. But the raw desire towards that 70% discount, with cashback on top of it, makes you feel that you would be stupid to miss out. The thrill isn't in the deal alone but in the *expectation* that you're gaming the system and stealing a deal. Before you know it, you've bought the headphones along with LED *mirchi* lights for a balcony you don't even have.

And it's not only eCommerce where this plays out, but also in gold loans. Muthoot Finance projects to be your partner by not only giving you money but also handing you a dream which holds promises of prosperity for your family and business. You just have to hand over your gold, and your life will turn around. The reality may not be as shiny, but the expectation is surely 24 karat.

That's the magic of the *Expectancy-Value Theory* in action. As long as you can make consumers expect something exciting, you've partially won. Whether it holds up to that promise or not is secondary; *important, but secondary.* The real sale happens much before she taps "add to cart." After all, like Red says in

Shawshank Redemption: "Hope is a good thing, maybe the best of things."

Why You End Up Buying Things You Don't Need: Impulse Buying

The genius of impulse buying is that some brands can ignite that little voice in your head that says, "I must have this now!" - almost at will.

In our malls, which have become temples of temptation in themselves, impulse buying has evolved into an art form. Let's start with Reliance Fresh, the home of "I'll just grab a few things." You walk in wanting to buy toothpaste and some milk, and you walk out with your cart, looking like you're stockpiling for the next lockdown. Why? Because retailers have strategically stacked their shelves with shiny, discounted items at every nook and corner. "Buy me NOW!" they silently scream to you, and you toss another jumbo pack of masala peanuts into your cart.

And then comes the climax: the bill counter ambush - when you least expect it. You're happy after your shopping spree, and suddenly, you're hit with another shelf of chocolate bars, condoms and "limited edition" mints. This is where impulse buying is at its strongest. The items on offer are low cost and low risk, and your brain's already tired from the labyrinth of groceries it navigated, so it just gives in. So you toss two Dairy Milks and one Coke Zero into your cart. You didn't have any need, but you went ahead anyway.

And that's the interesting bit: it's never about what you need. It's about the rush of discovering something new that you didn't know you wanted. And by the time you leave Reliance Fresh, you're the proud owner of a new kitchen appliance, a needless showpiece for your drawing room and a lifetime supply of *masala kaju* - all thanks to some clever visual merchandising and some neat psychological tricks.

TURN INSIGHTS INTO ACTION

→ Intrinsic motivation

- ◆ Slowly build authentic communities (like Harley Davidson) and position your brand as a lifestyle which customers can connect with

- ◆ Create value-driven campaigns that touch consumers' personal values (e.g. sustainability)

→ Extrinsic motivation

- ◆ Offer time-sensitive deals like flash sales to trigger urgency.

- ◆ Create gamified loyalty programs with a transparent path to rewards (e.g. Starbucks)

→ Theory of Planned Behaviour

- ◆ Simplify checkout with one-click payments (e.g. Amazon)

- ◆ Lower the customer's perceived risk by offering trials and flexible EMIs

→ Expectancy-Value Theory

- ◆ Show tangible value and potential benefits clearly in your communication - Showcase testimonials of people who can trigger similar expectations.

→ Impulse Buying

  ◆ Strategically place low-risk and high-desire items near checkout counters or "people also bought" sections in the checkout flow.

4.

ATTENTION

The New Oil

Confession Time. You've lost hours of your life to doom-scrolling on your smartphone, right? And I am not talking about the kind of doom-scrolling which acts as a stress reliever after a hard day's work. I am talking about the kind of vortex that starts with a notification of a meme sent by a friend and ends up being two hours spent on Instagram Reels. You didn't plan this, but somehow it just happened. Why?

These kinds of experiences are at the heart of what's now called the *attention economy*. Attention is the new oil, and yours is being extracted and sold to the highest bidder. Brands, apps, and influencers are not coming for your wallet alone; they want something far more dearer: your undivided attention. In the economy of eyeballs, every second could be a fortune.

But why exactly is our attention so valuable? Everyone wants you to watch *their* ad, download *their* app, and click *their* link. So, in this kind of world, your attention is the most scarce and highly coveted resource. It's like every time you scroll, brands start waving their hands in the air, hoping that you'll glance at them. Because whenever you pay attention, they'll convert that into engagement and then sales and then loyalty.

Understanding How Attention Works

Selective Attention Theory

Imagine you're in an Ola cab, it's rush hour, and you're scrambling to get to the office. Windows are rolled up, and yet you can hear horns blaring. Your driver has a mildly disturbing fondness for early 90s Hindi film music and has got Kumar Sanu cranked up on high volume. Yet somehow, in this chaos, the slightest 'ting' from your phone cuts through the noise. You recognise your notification tone very well, and your brain actively looks out for it, like an alert security guard. You open your phone. Is it from him/her? Is it that recruiter emailing back? Nah, it's a notification from Swiggy for 20% off your breakfast order. Anticlimax, but how did it all happen?

This is what is called *selective attention*. Our brains have a sophisticated filter that kind of tunes out the noise and Kumar Sanu's singing to zoom in on what really matters. Like a notification from Swiggy when we're *actually* quite hungry. This is how apps like Swiggy and Zomato speak into our brains at exactly the right moment. They know when to ping you when you've rushed out of your home and didn't get the chance to grab breakfast. They've mastered the art of interrupting your life in the most relevant and valuable way possible.

Selective attention works beautifully in apps like Google Maps. Think about it - you're driving, and your friend in the passenger seat is talking loudly with you, yet when Google Maps says, "Turn left in 500 meters", you immediately snap back to attention. Why does this happen? Because it's important information for the immediate goal in front of you - reaching your destination via maps. Everything else temporarily becomes white noise, and all you care about is turning left. They never bombard you with notifications but only talk to you at the moment of highest relevance, when you give them a disproportionate share of your attention.

Broadbent's Filter Model

Our brain is probably like a strict bouncer outside a posh South Delhi nightclub, deciding who gets in and who doesn't. It's a skilful gatekeeper which only lets the most important and relevant information pass through and denies entry to all the other kinds of noise. But even the best bouncers sometimes take a smoke break, and this is when marketers like to sneak in past the velvet rope and make a mark.

That's *Broadbent's Filter Model*. Our brains are presented with a humungous amount of stimuli every second, and if it didn't filter out most of it, we would die of sensory overload.

Take a simple example: you're walking down Connaught Place. There are people chatting, vendors selling, cabs honking. But your brain has tuned out most of it because you're looking for a specific cafe. But as you're walking, suddenly you see a large, red sign that says "*100 rupaye mein mobile cover.*" Suddenly, all else blurs, and that cafe can wait a minute longer. Your brain sees that sign and filters out all the noise again. Why? Because you've been thinking about replacing your old, worn-out mobile cover for a while, and this doesn't seem like a bad deal at all.

This is how the model plays out in real life. When our brains filter out most of the information thrown at us, somehow, they find a small opening to slide their message in and make us buy when our filter is at its weakest.

Treisman's Attenuation Model

But sometimes your attention is divided, right? What happens then? Like the moments when you're half-watching TV, half-scrolling through Instagram, and half-thinking about your Zomato order that's on the way (yes, that's three halves - math is no match for the truly distracted). Treisman's Attenuation Model talks about how we process information even when we're not 100% paying attention.

Nothing is ever completely blocked out. Some things are just turned down in volume, waiting in the wings to spring back up when your brain gets distracted. It's like your mind juggling many balls in the air, but it gives priority to the one that's most important at this very moment while the less important ones are in the air, in the background.

Treisman's model is quite different from Broadbent's. While Broadbent argues that less important stuff is filtered out, Treisman says that it's never completely filtered out; it just gets turned down. Your brain knows that it's there, but on a low volume, waiting to catch your interest and attention again.

Kahneman's Capacity Model

Our brains are not exactly the tireless supercomputers that we sometimes wish that they were. They're more like over-worked and sometimes tipsy corporate *mazdoors*, trying to empty their inbox at the end of a tough day. And like every other corporate *mazdoor*, they have their limits. Brains can only process so much information before they start falling apart at the seams. This is where it's important to know how Kahneman's Capacity Model works.

In simple terms, Daniel Kahneman says that your attention is a finite resource. You've only got a certain amount of brainpower to invest, and once that's used up, you're pretty much running on fumes. It's like having one bucket of water to fill up a dozen pots - you're never going to fill them all. You've probably experienced this at some point - you're juggling WhatsApp texts while a Netflix documentary is on, half-listening to your partner talk about how their day went while you have 20 open tabs on your laptop where you were looking for Airbnbs for your next weekend getaway. What's happening here exactly? You're spread thin, like a little butter on too much bread. And something will slip for sure - most probably your conversation with your partner (we've all suffered terrible consequences after).

Brands and marketers use this well. They know that beyond a point, they need to make their ads, pitches and UI/UX as *low effort* as possible so that their message and utility slip into your mental stream when you've got the cognitive capacity of a rabbit.

Take the example of booking an Uber. You were at a party, it got late, and you had a few too many gulab jamuns (or, let's be honest, a few too many beers). You're tired and tipsy, and your cognitive capacities are pretty numb. You just want to get home. Here's when Uber's friction-free UI/UX shines. One tap on the pre-saved address under "Home", and it starts looking for drivers nearby. Minimum number of actions to get to the user goal - booking a cab and getting into one. Uber has stripped this process to bare essentials because they know that when you're getting back home drunk or thinking about your morning presentation after burning the midnight oil, you're running on mental fumes. And at times like this, you don't like complexity - you want *ease*.

Kahneman's model confirms that our brains fundamentally want to conserve energy. Product managers know that they've got to make their product experience seamless and simple, and marketers know that they've got to keep it simple in their communication at times when the user's capacity to process is depleted.

Attention will always be a finite resource, and it's up to the marketer to understand at which point in the consumer journey exactly how much fuel they've got left in their mental tank - so that they can tailor their messaging accordingly.

How Do Humans Allocate Attention?

Intrinsic factors: what you care about

You're obviously going to pay more attention to things that really matter to you. If you've been wanting to buy a new smartphone and, out of nowhere, see an ad from Samsung Galaxy, you will surely pay attention because you're in the market for a new phone. And this is where brands like Amazon play. From your search and browsing history, they know exactly what you're in the market for, and they'll find a way to put it in front of you super casually.

But it's not only about what you're interested in; it's also about what feels *timely*. Whenever you spend some time looking for your next hotel in Goa on MakeMyTrip - within hours, your Instagram feed starts showing ads from luxury hotels in Goa, adventure packages and "last-minute deals." They know that you've *kind of* made up your mind to go to Goa, and this is when they pounce - to turn your fleeting curiosity into a proper booking on their portal.

Extrinsic Factors: Shiny objects get more attention

Then there are the majority - marketers trying to pull your attention, regardless of what your personal interests are at the time. Walk down any street in your neighborhood, and you'll see neon signs, billboards (often digital ones), and gaudy shop fronts, all screaming and begging for your attention. Which are the brands that stand out? The ones that create true novelty and disrupt the flow of sameness. Whether it's the giant yellow "SALE" banner outside Zudio or Ranveer Singh in an action shot on a Thums Up hoarding - brands use every tool in the book to get you to stop, notice and pay attention.

Emotional and Psychological factors: playing with feelings

The ultimate hack remains playing with emotions, no matter how bad that sounds. Nothing grabs attention as well as something that makes you *feel* something. That's why brands like Cadbury Dairy Milk make their Diwali ads in a certain way. They want to bring out the feeling of family, togetherness, warmth and tradition rather than just talking about how yummy their chocolate is. And the moment you feel something - happiness, nostalgia or even fear - your attention is locked in.

Why does Spotify do better than other apps which do the exact same thing? Even when most competitors are much cheaper. It's because they've cracked how to serve you music based on your *mood*. Feeling reflective today? Here's a moody, slow playlist that reflects that mood. Feeling pumped during that gym session on a Friday morning? They've got a high-energy playlist. Their secret sauce is their ability to tap into your emotional state, thus grabbing not only your attention but also tailoring the experience so that you keep coming back for more.

How Do Marketers Hack Our Attention?

Visual Attention

It's often all about visuals. Our brains process pictures faster than words. This is why you see Amazon India relying on over-the-top, big, bold imagery during their Great Indian Festival. Everything is oversized - giant fonts, flashy banners, discounts in bright colors. Why? Because our brains can't help but stop to notice. We're drawn to contrast and novelty, and Amazon likes to throw everything at you to see what sticks. To be honest, I never liked the elephants in that logo.

Zudio does this when you enter their stores. The biggest, brightest offers are placed right at the front of the store. Because you can't escape it, it's designed to hijack your attention when you're passing by to make sure that you walk in.

Auditory Attention: Washing Power Nirma

Indians love jingles. Why do you think brands like Airtel and Amul Macho (*yeh toh bada toing hai*) spent so much time perfecting the audio in the ads? Because even if you forget the brand for a bit, it's almost impossible to get their irritating tunes out of your head. Whether it's '*Har ek friend zaruri hota hai*' or '*washing powder nirma*' - it's the same strategy.

That annoying earworm overstays their welcome in your ears. Nima Rose, Lifebuoy, Vicco Vajradanti - I am sure you sang the jingles in your head while reading their names. They've somehow *wormed* their way into our subconscious so that the next time we're thinking about buying a soap or toothpaste, some of these brands are the first to pop up in our heads. The fact that it's annoying doesn't matter; it works.

Grabbing attention through flash, bang and celebrity

When subtlety fails, brands bring out the heavy guns - flash, bang and celebrity. These are three known tactics for not just nudging your attention but grabbing it by the collar.

First, *flash*. If you want someone to look, make it impossible not to. Think of the loud neon sign saying '*Fresh Baked Bread*' in front of every Subway. Or the loud SALE banners you see plastered everywhere in malls. "*Last Few items left!*" written in red - messages like these work because your brain is hardwired to notice contrast, novelty and FOMO.

Then there's *bang*. This is a weapon that's hard for us to tune out. Walk through a local market, and suddenly, a loudspeaker blares: "*Buy One Get One, only for today.*" It cuts through the noise, and your brain can't help but listen and take one look. Ads for products like Coca Cola and Lay's feature fizzy and crunchy sounds. They want you to not just see the ad but *to feel* it and then want their product.

Finally, *celebrity*. Nothing hacks attention more than a familiar face that you find aspirational - whether it's Virat Kohli selling Puma or Deepika Padukone selling Tanishq. We like to believe that celebrity endorsements don't work on us - but they do. Celebrities bring instant trust, credibility and attention to a brand. You might not care about the Diptique and Dunhill perfume combo - but once you know that King Khan wears it, you're suddenly curious.

Flash, bang and celebrity don't ask for attention; they just take it. And once they've got yours, good luck looking away.

Attention Blindness

This is one of life's cruel jokes. You could be staring directly at something and not see it at all. Your brain is efficient, but sometimes too efficient for its own good. It often filters out what it deems irrelevant so that you're blissfully unaware of what's right in front of you.

Think about standing in front of the toothpaste aisle at D-Mart; you were so busy choosing between "whitening" and "tartar control" that you totally missed the giant BOGO sign hanging right in front of you and missed the deal. Or at the airport, when you're laser-focused on finding your green suitcase on the luggage belt, and you completely miss the announcement that your flight's luggage has been transferred to a different belt altogether.

If you've ever commuted by a Mumbai local, then you know this. There's a huge insurance ad right above your head, but you're busy getting a full-body massage from your co-passengers (*without consent*). The poster is invisible to you until the moment when your attention wavers for a second, and then you see it. Brands don't need 100% of your attention; they just have to wait for the moment you let your guard down.

The Ethics (or Lack of Ethics) of Harvesting Attention

At what point does hacking attention cross the line into pure manipulation? Apps like Instagram and X are designed to make you scroll endlessly. They don't want just seconds of your attention like some other brands do; they want *hours*. And they won't stop at using all possible psychological tricks for you to do so.

Some apps are worse; they use what are called "dark patterns" to keep you hooked. Have you ever tried unsubscribing from a service, but it was impossible to find the cancel button? That's an intentional dark pattern - making it confusing and difficult for the user to leave.

Marketers have always been in the business of grabbing attention and using it to persuade you. But the stakes have just gotten higher in the current age. At what point does it stop being about selling a product and start being about exploiting your mental weaknesses for commercial gain?

Brands, apps, and platforms will continue to compete for our attention, and more so in the coming years and decades. But it's for all of us to understand the costs. Users need to ask that once their attention is harvested for the highest bidder - what are they getting in return?

In the end, it should be up to the consumer to decide how much attention they want to pay and to whom.

TURN INSIGHTS INTO ACTION

- → Selective Attention Theory

  - ◆ Use contextual triggers (e.g. meal time push notifications from Swiggy) to target relevant moments

- → Broadbent's Filter Model

  - ◆ Place ads in natural lulls (e.g. between non-powerplay overs in cricket matches) to benefit from attention gaps

- → Treisman's Attenuation Model

  - ◆ Keep subtle, persistent messaging that can pop up into the consumer's attention later (e.g. background banners in stores)

- → Kahneman's Capacity Model

  - ◆ Use minimal, easy-to-use interfaces to reduce cognitive load and eliminate the need for user action (Netflix's next episode autoplay)

- → Visual Attention

  - ◆ Look at eye-tracking data to figure out where to put key elements (like the CTA button) on your landing pages

→ Auditory Attention

- Nothing works like jingles that get into your head - create memorable audio cues. Consider sonic branding for your logo.

→ Attentional Blindness

- Place your ads at unexpected spots with a simplified visual hierarchy so that it reduces distractions and makes the consumer focus on what matters

5.

CHOICE

Do We Even Have a Choice?

Choice is perhaps the most seductive lie told in the world of modern capitalism. We are made to believe that we live in a world where the consumer is king, and she is empowered to choose from an endless array of choices. But if you have ever scrolled through Swiggy for 20 minutes only to order the same biryani again, you know that this brand of "freedom" feels less like a choice and more like a chore. The main paradox of choice is that - the more options we have, the less free we feel.

Take a stroll down any supermarket, and you'll be greeted with a heady dose of *choice overload*. You're looking for a basic toothpaste, and you're overwhelmed by the breadth of choice available. Whitening, herbal, cavity protection, charcoal, fluoride-free and something strangely Ayurvedic that your grandmom would swear by. But what happens at the end? You pick up the same Colgate Total that your family has been using for decades.

And that's the main issue - the more choices we're given, the more we try to revert to what's familiar and known. Brands have caught onto this behavior of ours where we reduce cognitive load. They know that when you're offered a dizzying array of options, you may feel less in control and hence revert to the same tried-and-tested brands that you always buy. Big market leaders use this trick to defend market share.

Too Much of a Good Thing: Choice Overload

Like the experience of buying toothpaste above, we just hate being thrown into the deep end of the choice pool. When you step away from the toothpaste aisle and go to the one with snacks - the same story plays out with chips: salted, peri-peri, cream and onion, baked, popped. There's even a healthy variant made out of quinoa. By the time you weigh the options and figure out the balance between indulgence and guilt reduction - you're left wondering why you didn't just stick with your regular *Lay's Magic Masala*.

Too much of any good thing is always exhausting. Our brains aren't designed to navigate so many choices. We face decision paralysis or, worse, the regret which comes after a hurried choice. So, we just try to avoid the maze of too many possibilities and stick with the known devil.

Back in the day, when you went to *paan* shops, you had two standard options, *meetha* and tobacco-filled ones. Fast forward to today when there are chocolate paans, ice paans, fire paans (yes, that's a thing), paan with avocados, paan dipped in exotic syrups and whatnot. You stick to your usual classic *meetha* paan and are left wondering if chocolate paan was the wiser choice.

The sad reality is that too many choices rob us of the satisfaction of having made the best choice. We spend too much energy deciding what we want, and then we're too exhausted to enjoy what we chose and are left thinking if the other one would have been better.

Maximizers vs. Satisficers: The Two Kinds of Shoppers

If you over-generalize, there are only two kinds of shoppers out there: maximizers and satisficers. *Maximizers* are typical perfectionists. They need to go to the depths of each option, look at every detail, and read every review before they make their decision. The result? Often, it's exhaustion, anxiety and buyer's remorse.

They're the ones who'll spend hours scrolling through Myntra, trying to find the best kurta for their perfect festive look. The irony is that after all that effort, they will still be less satisfied with their purchase. They'll wonder if they should have gone for the handloom one, the linen one or the one with the fancy neckline. The grass is always greener for a Maximizer - especially when they trap themselves on the other side.

Satisficers are on the opposite end of the spectrum. They're what you would call "chill-pills." They don't need the best option; they're only looking for a 'good enough' one. They can walk into an Adidas store, pick up the first decent pair of shoes that fit well and head straight to the cash counter. No comparisons, no agony. They know that there is no such thing as the perfect choice, and that's perfectly alright.

If Only We Were Rational Beings: Rational Choice Theory

The *rational choice theory* was put forward by Gary Becker in the 1960s, and it suggests that we take perfectly rational and logical decisions to get the best possible outcome. Which is great in theory, but reality has other plans. Practically, emotion beats logic almost every time.

Think about car shopping. You'd assume buyers carefully weigh mileage, maintenance costs, safety, accessories, etc. Yes, they do, but they're more swayed by the rugged image of the Mahindra Thar, even though most will never take it off-road. Emotion, status and identity shape the choice, and then the customer justifies the choice with utility-based functional specifications and benefits.

Take Tanishq, for example. An expensive gold necklace bought for a wedding doesn't make the best logical sense. Gold jewelry has very little utility as an investment (there are way better financial instruments like ETFs to capture the price upside). But emotionally, it's priceless. And that's how the Rational Choice Theory fails in the real world.

The Limits of Our Decision-Making: Bounded Rationality

Herbert Simon, back in the 1950s, gave us the idea of *Bounded Rationality*, which basically means that we're not walking calculators who logically optimize every decision. But we're human beings who make choices that are often just *good enough*. And thank god for that. Otherwise, we would be stuck choosing toothpaste at supermarket aisles forever.

When you walk into a *Woodland*, you want a pair of shoes that are rugged and durable. You start quite properly by comparing leather quality, durability, sole grip, etc. But after trying on your fifth pair, you've had enough, and you just want something that's good enough for your next hiking trip. It needs to be comfortable enough, within your budget, and, most importantly - available in your size. That's about it. Did you get the perfect hiking shoes? Who knows. But will it take you up the mountain? Yes! And that's all you care about.

In a world exploding with choices, Bounded Rationality keeps us sane. It's not about finding that perfect option but finding the one that's good enough in the shortest amount of time. Because, let's face it, often "good enough" is more than enough.

How Store Layouts and Design Influence Choice

When I switched from consumer electronics to luxury retail, I found the entire emphasis on visual merchandising quite fascinating. The level to which the sights, sounds, smells and placement of stores would be planned and maintained; everything from the lighting to the props was supposed to make you think that it's perfectly normal to splurge ₹30,000 on a pair of denim.

Store layout is retail's puppet master that massively influences choice. It guides your eyes and ultimately makes you pull out your credit card faster. Thought you had come in only for a quick glance? Think again. By the time you leave, you will have spent way more than last month's groceries.

Take *Nature's Basket*, a pilgrimage destination for people who can name more than five kinds of cheese. You could step in thinking that you just need a nice loaf of bread and some butter. But the store's masterful layout leads you past shelves stocked with fancier cheeses, global spices and truffle oils. Before you know it, you've put smoked paprika in your basket for the pasta you might end up making only once. The design inside creates walking pathways that nudge you to think that you deserve a little indulgence and you should eat higher-quality ingredients.

Now, let's imagine walking into *Malabar Gold & Diamonds*. Their store layout and design have one objective: to make every piece feel special and, by extension, to make you feel special for choosing it. Their signature sets are showcased under soft, flattering light, making them look divine. Each section is separated by style and occasion - wedding jewelry, daily wear, men's etc. You just glide through the layout and walk out, having spent a bomb.

The trick is clever. Retailers don't just want you to walk in and out; they want you to experience the store like an art exhibition. By the time you reach the exit, you have gone from "just one thing" to "maybe one more."

That's the magic of visual merchandising and store design - an amazing tool to influence shopper choice.

Weighing the Options: Multi-Attribute Utility Theory (MAUT)

MAUT (*I love this acronym*) is just a fancy way of saying that we evaluate products based on multiple attributes and pick the one that has the best combination of attributes and gives us the best balance; like creating a mental pros and cons list for a purchase.

This could be for deciding if you should leave your current job and take the next one or if you should buy that swanky SUV in cash or take out a loan. These kinds of problems share a common feature - decision alternatives impact multiple attributes. The attractiveness of each choice will be a function of how well it scores on each of the attributes that are important and also the relative importance of each attribute.

For example, when you're buying a smartphone, you might weigh how well it does on features like camera quality, battery life and price. However, not all attributes are equally important for every unique customer. The decision-making has to weigh how well the brand does in each of these features and the relative importance of each feature to the customer's unique use case.

MAUT (*I'll repeat the acronym once again for fun*) tells us that a customer's choice is often just a balancing act. We don't over-index on one factor but evaluate several to ensure that we get the maximum utility out of our purchase.

How the Past Shapes Our Present Decisions

Our memory guides and shapes the choices that we make. Whatever we remember about our past experiences, whether it's good or bad or ugly, influences what we choose in the present. But the important thing to note here is that our memories are not always accurate.

Take eating out, for example. You might remember having a great time at Barbeque Nation because the last time you were there, you were celebrating a colleague's promotion, and there was fun and laughter. So, what you're recalling fondly about the place is not the food but the company and vibes. So, the next time you're looking for a place to go out as a group, Barbeque Nation instantly pops up in your mind.

This is why brands invest so heavily in creating memorable experiences for their customers. This is because they know that you'll recall how you *felt* more than the product or service itself.

Choice Architecture

This concept was popularized by Thaler and Sunstein in their 2008 book *Nudge*, which tells us that how the options are presented has a dramatic effect on how we make decisions. Small changes in how choices are framed can steer us towards a certain choice without us realizing it.

Remember when you last ordered food from Swiggy? The app presents certain restaurants as "Best for Biryani" and certain dishes as "best sellers." You are way more likely to choose from these options simply because they're put in front of you as popular, safe and liked by others. That's the nudge. The food you choose feels like your own decision, but in reality, Swiggy softly pushes you in the direction of certain restaurants and certain dishes.

Another example is when you finish placing your order at McDonald's; the order-taker asks you if you want fries with that for 'just a few extra rupees.' They present the option to upgrade as an easy, affordable and no-brainer option. It feels like a small win because it's framed as value.

Then, there's a very clever use of what are called "default options." When you're booking a flight through MakeMyTrip, for example, the travel insurance option is pre-selected for you. This default selection gently pushes you to go for services which you might have otherwise skipped if it required you to actively choose them. But since it's pre-selected, a large section of people just go along without making any deliberate deselection. Choice Architecture is about structuring your choices in such a way that consumers are nudged towards the ones that you want them to choose. Whether it's a default option, packaging that makes certain claims or push notifications to renew - the way choices are framed ultimately dictates the choices that we end up making.

TURN INSIGHTS INTO ACTION

→ Choice overload

- Limit the number of choices to avoid overwhelming customers

- Make it easier for them by highlighting some as "featured", "top sellers", or "editor's picks", etc.

→ Maximizers vs. Satisficers

- Make detailed information and comparisons available for maximizers and quick buy options or 'no-brainer' deals available for satisficers

→ Rational Choice Theory & Bounded Rationality

- Bring out cost savings or long-term benefits along with side-by-side comparisons of your product with competitors

→ Store Layout and design

- Place high-value items in higher traffic areas where customer dwell time is likely to be higher

- Use lighting, music and color schemes that create an urgency to buy (there's tons of research out there for this)

→ Multi-Attribute Utility Theory

- Bring out different feature bundles for different customer use cases (some may value durability most, while others may value aesthetics in the same product)

→ Choice Architecture

♦ Pre-select optimal choices like warranties or insurance to make the customer's journey frictionless

6.

COGNITIVE BIASES

Our Invisible Puppeteers

Cognitive biases are those voices inside your head that constantly influence your decisions without you noticing them much. You think that you make your decisions independently, but in reality, a complex system of mental shortcuts pulls you towards your decisions. Like a magician doing tricks inside your head - so let us go backstage and see how all this happens.

If, as a marketer, you understand how cognitive biases work, then that sets you apart from 90% of your peers. But knowing how to wield their power puts you in the 99th percentile of marketers. Biases like these show up in each step of the consumer journey - from when they pick up our product (or the competitor's), when they decide to pay, and when they evaluate if they made the right decision.

If you've come across this popular book called *Thinking Fast & Slow* by Daniel Kahneman, then you may have heard about the concept of System 1 and System 2 thinking. Let's break down how this works in the ultimate battleground for marketers - your brain. System 1 can be seen as a parallel to the reptilian brain, which is fast and impulsive, and System 2 can be seen as the new brain, which is slow and deliberate. System 1 will drive your impulsive purchases, but System 2 will be the party pooper that forces you to open an Excel sheet and weigh the pros and cons. Marketers try to excite your System 1 with ads which trigger their emotions but also give just the right amount of data to keep your System 2 from feeling ignored.

The interplay between systems like these and many other eccentricities that our brain has, creates the foundation for cognitive biases to exist. Only by truly understanding and applying them can brands rule over minds, hearts and wallets.

Anchoring Bias

You're wandering in Crawford Market in Mumbai, and you see this stunning handwoven rug that looks like hundreds of hours have gone into its making (or so the shopkeeper would have you believe). You ask for the price, and he says that he can give it to you for ₹10,000. You act as shocked as someone who has heard that the sun rose in the west today. But then you deploy your bargaining chops and finally close the deal at ₹4,000. You feel like you've got an amazing deal because your mind's still anchored to the price of ₹10,000. That carpet could be worth ₹2,000, but that doesn't matter.

Anchoring bias is the mental shortcut where the first piece of information that we receive (price, fact, etc.) becomes the reference point against which we compare all subsequent information. eCommerce players use this well by striking off the fictitious price of ₹5,000 for the dress and making you feel that you've got a steal at 70% when you paid ₹1,500. Even if the discounted price is more than what you originally wanted to pay, it doesn't matter - you got something at 70% off! Your brain still clings to that notional figure of ₹5,000.

Even when you're looking at real estate listings on MagicBricks, the first few results on your search will always be the more expensive ones so that a few scrolls down - everything starts looking like a deal.

Confirmation Bias

You're picking your fantasy team on Dream11 and you, of course, pick Virat Kohli - even though his form of late hasn't been the best. Why? Because he's your favorite, and you hope against hope that in this next match, he will get a ton and silence his critics. Your brain wants to try and confirm what it already believes. That's *confirmation bias*, where you look for information that somehow supports your pre-existing beliefs while consciously ignoring all data to the contrary. The app also shows you players you have historically chosen to further play into this bias.

Amazon knows that sometimes you've mentally decided to buy that JBL speaker even before you head to the reviews. So, the positive 5-star reviews will be on top, which confirms how amazing the speaker looks and sounds. The 1-star reviews? Oh, those must be from folks who had a bad delivery experience because the product seems perfect.

Hick's Law

The problem with walking inside a Croma is the sheer number of choices, which often feels overwhelming. If I want a new TV, I am standing in front of a giant wall full of TVs, and to be honest, most of them look the same. There's a big one, a very big one, and a ridiculously big one. But when the salesperson starts talking about the specs, pixel density, refresh rate, latency, HDR… you're suddenly paralyzed in your decision to find the best one. You now just want to know which one's the best to watch YouTube on.

Hick's Law says that the more choices you are given, the longer it will take for you to come to a decision and the less satisfied you'll be with it. That's why Swiggy makes your life slightly easier by not bombarding you with messaging from the 300 restaurants around you that are delivering, but it only nudges you towards the ones that you may like based on your previous ordering patterns. They understand that when you're hungry, triggering Hick's Law is the worst thing that can happen, so they show on top the places that you most often order from to play on familiarity.

Priming

You're going out for lunch, and you walk past this amazing hoarding of Deepika Padukone gulping down a fizzy and refreshing Coca Cola. You get to the restaurant and order chicken wings, and when the server asks you if you want Coke with that, you quickly say, "Yes, of course". That's *priming* in action. Exposure to one stimulus has a large impact on how you respond to another stimulus after that.

You see an attractive banner when you open the Myntra app, with good-looking, happy people in festive wear. So, even though you came to buy a new pair of boxers, you can't help but browse through the ethnic section for kurtas just once.

Priming shapes expectations and tells us that prior exposure to the right kind of images, colors, sounds, etc., can marinate us towards deciding to buy when asked, like one gentle push.

The Decoy Effect

I always disliked the names Starbucks gives to the S, M, L sizes of their drinks - Tall, Grande and Venti. The tall's too small, the venti's too big - but the grande? That's perfect. They play the decoy effect very well. They just have a less attractive option, which is the decoy, to make the middle option look like the best deal. And that's what they originally wanted to sell, too.

All subscription-based businesses like Netflix do the same thing. They'll have one super basic plan, which doesn't have all that you need. Then, a fully packed plan, which is expensive but has everything and more. But then there's the plan in the middle, which is cheaper than the highest one but has everything you need. The decoys to the left (or right) may not be meant to be chosen at all. They always wanted you to see value in the middle option and go for it.

The decoy effect plays on our need to evaluate and make the highest ROI choice. It's a game of perception, really - but once you understand it, you start spotting the decoys easily.

Loss Aversion

You don't want to lose it all, and you fear that like nothing else. Because the fear of losing is always greater than the joy of winning. This is why most Indian wealth (outside of real estate and gold) is locked in inefficient fixed deposits in banks. For our parents' generation, at least, the fear of losing money was far greater than the lure of better returns on their capital.

This is why brands offer free trials and money-back guarantees to make sure customers feel that even the worst-case scenario would mean that they don't lose any money. At Reliance Brands Limited, all luxury brands stores have a "no questions asked" return policy. When you're spending top bucks on a luxury handbag or shoes, you want to be reassured that your downside is protected and if something goes wrong, then the store will take care of it. That removes a big barrier to purchase.

Bandwagon Effect

Everyone around you starts talking about the new season of *Emily in Paris* and starts making references to dialogues from the new season, and you find yourself 'FOMOing' into watching it that weekend. That's the *bandwagon effect*. The more people do a thing, the more you are compelled to do it, even if you previously didn't want to.

Humans fundamentally want to conform to the herd because, in earlier times, straying far away from the herd meant death. Hence, we always want to be 'in-the-know' and 'with-the-times'. Social proof is also a manifestation of the bandwagon effect. If others like me have liked a product, then there's a high chance that I might like it too.

Halo Effect

I was watching the new IDFC Bank ads with Amitabh Bachchan in them. I don't know much about the bank at all, to be honest. But something about Big-B being there accords a dash of trust to the bank. He's been a credible voice for decades, and I'm sure he won't promote a fly-by-night bank just to make a few extra bucks. That's the halo that Mr. Bachchan casts.

We keep saying that celebrity endorsements don't work for us, and yet the biggest chunks of marketing money keep going to Virat, Ranveer, and Deepika. The *halo effect* isn't just about celebrities. If you see a new D2C website with a sleek layout and well-shot product imagery, you're far more likely to trust their products and pay a premium to try them due to the halo they've managed to create. The Halo Effect is like cognitive glitter - once it's sprinkled over something, it starts sparkling.

Fitt's Law

When Ola takes a while to find a cab for you, and you decide to cancel and take a rickshaw instead, you find two options when you ask to cancel: Big Bold - "*Keep*

Looking" and in slightly lighter and smaller font - "*Cancel instead.*" You're more likely to press the big, bold one even if you originally wanted to press the other. That's what Fitt's Law tells us - the size and prominence of certain objects determine how well and fast we interact with them.

On all eCommerce apps, the "Buy Now" button is more prominent than the "Add to Cart" one. They want you to proceed to payment in the fewest possible steps.

Even when you walk into a supermarket, the most eye-catching merchandise is kept at your eye level. The stuff they don't want to sell as much is kept on the bottom shelves. It's about making it as easy for the customer as possible and making sure that they don't have to put any physical or mental effort into buying.

Nudge Theory

Small changes in things around us can guide us towards better choices without making us feel restricted in any way. That's what Thaler and Sunstein said in their 2008 book *Nudge*. In the last chapter, we discussed that we can very effectively be nudged when making a decision if the brand seems like a friendly stranger. And the opposite happens when we perceive the brand to be like a pushy credit card salesman at the mall.

Zomato labels some dishes as 'Healthy', often with calorie counts. While you still may go for that cheese-burst pizza, sometimes that nudge would be enough to make you choose the salad instead. They made you feel good about making a healthier choice without pushing you in any way.

When you book a ticket through BookMyShow, they nudge you by pre-selecting a ₹1 donation to their charity BookAChange. It's not a hard push, you can easily opt-out with one tap, but it gently steers you into doing some good.

Availability Heuristic

You're deciding where to take your partner for a date, and you consider Restaurants A and B - both are amazing options in all respects, but you remember that the last time you were at B, you had to wait 20 minutes to get your car back from the valet. Hence, you pick restaurant A. The availability heuristic tells us that our brains are influenced heavily by singular occurrences that we remember when compared to less memorable ones.

The issue with the availability heuristic is that easily recallable memories, such as the long valet wait, may not be sufficient in truly evaluating if an experience like that is likely to repeat itself. Hence, we often make less-than-optimal decisions.

You see way too many ads from Neeman's shoes all over your Instagram feed. So when you're in the market for new comfy loafers and the store's right in front of you - you walk in and get two pairs. Neeman's was top-of-mind, and in marketing, there's no currency as valuable.

Reactance

When you see a prompt near the 'Buy Now' button that says 'only 1 item left' or when there's a timer on the masthead of the website that says 'Sale ends in 01 hour: 51 minutes' - that sudden urge and urgency that you feel, that's a function of reactance. Reactance is your psychological response when you feel that your ability or freedom to decide is being restricted. And this makes you do things that you didn't quite plan to do.

When eCommerce players do limited-edition sneaker drops or flash sales, reactance is triggered. You feel like someone is poking scarcity and urgency at you; you know they're playing you, but you go ahead regardless (a touch of loss aversion is also at play here). Human beings love retaining their autonomy, or at least the perception of it. The moment a brand threatens to push you out of the driver's seat, you rebel by doing exactly what they want you to do.

Self-Serving Bias

When something works in your career, then it's because of your hard work, perseverance and grit. And, when something doesn't, it's the "external factors" like the market condition, the budget, the weather and whatnot. That's *self-serving bias* - our tendency to attribute success to internal factors and failure to external factors.

If your campaign does well, then you credit the sharp insight that came to you in a dream, and if it doesn't, then you do what any marketer has done in the generations that preceded you: you blame the agency.

Miller's Law

You're typing in your Aadhar number into a form for the third time, and somehow, you've forgotten it again. You just had it at the tip of your tongue, and now you don't. That's *Miller's Law* - which says that the average person can hold about seven items (plus or minus two) in their working memory. That's why OTPs mostly have six digits, so it's just secure enough and long enough for you to enter it correctly.

This is handy not only for marketers but also for UX designers. If you're creating landing pages or app interfaces, break down information into small, digestible pieces that are presented one at a time. If you have a form, have fewer fields presented to the user, one after the other, so that there is a perception of lesser effort. This is how Typeform uses progressive disclosure to give you one question at a time to keep it interesting and increase fill rates.

Labour Illusion

Whenever you fire up an app, and it gives you an interim screen which says *"finding the best options for you"* before showing your results, that's *labor illusion*. They could have shown you the search results immediately, but they chose to make you feel like a lot of work and customization has gone into presenting these results to you, and hence you should value them more. The illusion of effort makes it seem more special and 'made for you.'

When MakeMyTrip takes time and says, "searching for best prices", they've given you the illusion that they're scanning the vast expanse of the internet to get you the best deals. The longer it takes, the more convinced you are that the options in front of you are the best out there. Labour Illusion creates a perception that you're seeing the result of a vast network of computers (or people) working hard to give you the best choices, and that often works.

How Do We Become More Aware of the Biases That Shape Us?

There are hundreds of cognitive biases out there, way more than what we can cover in this chapter. You should check resources online to go down this rabbit hole. But what we need to talk about here is that, now that we know how marketers use biases like these to get you to do what they want, how do we use this knowledge to not get tricked?

Understanding how these biases work is Step-1 to recognizing that they are at play. This entire book is dedicated to helping us understand how we get played into buying more and more through the application of psychological theories which marketers have now weaponized against us.

I also must tell you that awareness will not make you immune. At least for me, it didn't. Cognitive biases are somehow deeply ingrained in our brains. It's almost impossible to train oneself to diffuse any attempt to use your biases against us. Sometimes, you can spot them, but more often than not, you won't be able to. What helps is pausing before making decisions that are truly important and asking oneself, "What biases could be at play here?" "How can I remove myself from this situation and be as objective as I need to be to make the most optimal decision?" By exercising that introspective muscle, we can at least stand a faint chance at becoming the masters of our own minds.

7.

PRICING

The Price Is Right, or Is It?

Pricing is sorcery. I don't think it's a simple number printed on a tag - but it's the cumulation of micro-strategies, testing, desires, perceptions and a whole lot more. There's more than what meets the eye.

Among the 4Ps of marketing, we marketers have always been obsessed with 'promotion' and thinking that 'price' is someone else's problem. But if you think about the consumer decision in totality, even the highest quality of promotion is likely to fall flat if the pricing is wrong. Price sets the tone for everything that the brand does. It's a clear declaration of the value that the consumer is expected to derive from the purchase. Think of price as a mini-salesperson itself.

We're the land of *'ek ke saath ek muft.'* Yet, we understand shockingly little about pricing as marketers. But that should change for you in the next hour or so.

Pricing Strategies That Are Known to Work

Charm Pricing

Why does ₹999 feel cheaper than ₹1,000? And why has Bata been doing this for decades? Our brain loves the "9" and uses the "left digit bias" to make us feel that it's almost a thousand, but not a thousand yet, which somehow works. There's enough research out there to prove that customers read from left to right with decreasing attention, and some wrongly interpret ₹475 as closer to ₹400 than ₹500 while hastily making a purchase. McDonald's still has McDeals at ₹99 to attract customers who are looking for a complete meal under a hundred rupees.

Prestige Pricing

This is the end of the price spectrum where the price tags are meant to be flaunted loud and proud. In higher-priced brands, it's less about what you pay and more about projecting that you have the *ability* to pay this much for something. A Sabyasachi lehenga isn't 20X better than an unbranded alternative, but the pricing sure seems to think so. They want you to feel like royalty when you splurge on being a Sabyasachi bride. You're basically paying for bragging rights. So, if it were more affordable, it would lose its allure - that's why it is priced to sustain the prestige associated with it.

Odd-Even Pricing

A Kama Ayurveda moisturizer at ₹2,500 vs one which is ₹2,497 - the latter seems cheaper and at a bargain. Odd prices are for bargain hunters who don't exactly like symmetrical prices as they seem un-discounted.

Anchoring and Adjustment

When you walk into Croma, the flagship TVs (75+ inches with the newest OLED screen) will be displayed first. When you see those giant TVs that cost lacs, the one that suits your drawing room - the 55" UHD one that costs ₹45,000- looks like a crazy deal. Once you're anchored to a higher price, everything starts getting compared to that initial reference point.

How Do We Actually Perceive Price?

Reference Price Theory

If you walk out of a Starbucks after having paid ₹450 for a cup of cappuccino, it seems 'standard', but if they served ₹250 masala chai, you would be up in arms. Reference prices in our heads act as an internal benchmark of what we think a product should cost. This is an average of our past experiences and exposures to that category. That's why when your Dad walks out after having a ₹250 masala chai, he tells you it was *'ekdum bakwaas'* because it clashes with the reference prices in his head and doesn't cross the price/value threshold.

Price-Quality Heuristic

Let's face it - we think that if it's expensive, there must be something good about it. It's embedded in our brains that "you get what you pay for." Hence, even without knowing or confirming the manufacturing practices or quality, we can conclude that the aloe vera gel from Forest Essentials at ₹1,500 is way more pure than what Patanjali sells for ₹90. Almost as if the Forest Essentials one was extracted by pious Himalayan maidens themselves.

If you're deciding which baby food to get for your toddler, you are likely to gravitate towards the one which is the most expensive since you want nothing but the best for your child, and price here becomes a powerful proxy for quality.

Price sensitivity & elasticity of demand

How we evaluate price increases depends largely on the category and context. If Maggi, which used to be ₹10 for most of our lives, becomes ₹15 - we're out with pitchforks. But if the new iPhone is ₹5,000 dearer than the last, even though not much has changed, we shrug and think of it as a few extra bucks on our EMI, nothing else. That's how differently we perceive price increases. If you remember your old economics lessons, you'll recall that for some categories, demand is inelastic, and for some, demand is elastic with respect to price changes. (Note: Google about Giffen and Veblen goods; it's an interesting rabbit hole).

Which Pricing Tricks Work on Us?

Bundling and Unbundling

If you've ever been to *Rajdhani* and had their amazing thalis, then you know that deals where everything's packed-in always feel like a bargain. When you get a JioFiber connection, you don't just get the internet services that you signed up for; to sweeten the deal, they throw in a bunch of OTT subscriptions, making it one 'no-brainer' package. You might not need all the services in the bundle, but who can refuse a good bargain?

Unbundling also works, however frustratingly. When you book an IndiGo flight, you have the option of adding a host of unbundled services beyond the basic flight ticket. You can add a meal, a preferred seat, quicker check-in, extra baggage allowance and a lot else. Everything has been morphed into a layer-by-layer pricing experience to make sure that your core purchase (the flight ticket) remains cheap and alluring.

Dynamic Pricing

Here, prices get adjusted in real-time based on the demand. Ola and Uber do it well, often ripping users off and fattening their bottom-lines. The moment it rains, prices surge faster than your heartbeat. But this is also known to happen in travel bookings, where you just saw the hotel at ₹5,700 per night, and it suddenly shoots up to ₹6,200 per night while you are browsing. The algorithm is meant to keep you on your toes and create a sense of urgency in getting you to convert.

Understanding Pricing Through the Lens of Behavioral Economics

Behavioral economics sounds like a fancy field of study, but it simply studies how humans behave when they make economic decisions. And pricing plays a big role here.

Mental Accounting

Richard Thaler gives us the concept of *mental accounting*, telling us how we allocate money to different "accounts" in our heads. We always have a vague "vacation fund" and a "Mahindra Thar fund" or a "new boots fund" in our heads. The fun starts when marketers start moving money around in your head across these accounts.

When you're booking a railway ticket through IRCTC, you don't mind paying ₹0.35 for railway insurance every time you book a ticket. Even if it was slightly more, not many people would deselect the option since insurance sits under the account labeled "safety" in your head.

Thaler's concept shows us how we see the same money differently due to perceptions in our heads. This could even extend to the ease of swiping ₹5,000 with a credit card vs. the pain of giving someone ten ₹500 notes and paying ₹5,000 in cash. The latter somehow feels more expensive.

The Pain of Paying

So, what you felt reading about handing over ₹5,000 in cash is what's called the "pain of paying." We just don't like parting with money. Not a surprise, right? This is the basis of the entire credit card industry. It doesn't pinch as much, somehow. Making a payment is not a completely rational act, as one might assume it to be. UPI payments feel frictionless when you're paying ₹15 for a samosa, versus giving the shopkeeper a ₹50 note and taking three tenners and one ₹5 coin back. FinTech companies are going one step further to remove the pain of paying by enabling contactless payments. That feels easier (and cheaper?) than entering your PIN for a transaction.

How Do You Give Discounts Without Pricing Yourself Cheaply?

Making discounts sound better through framing

Discounting is more about how you present prices than the quantum of the discount itself. "Flat 50%

off" feels very different from "Buy 1, Get 1 Free", even though mathematically, there may not be a meaningful difference.

During the 'Big Billion Days', when you see banners which say 'Up to 90% off', some distrust in your head says that most of the stuff will be 40% off and a handful of really bad, outdated items will be on 90% off. Good luck finding your size for those items. We've begun to detest sales which have the evil words "up to" next to them.

At DIESEL, we once ran two discounts: Flat ₹5,000 off on all denim in test markets while continuing to do a 25% off (which effectively comes to the same thing mathematically) in other markets. The price-off of ₹5,000 won, hands down, as the same discount, was framed in a much more valuable way.

Endowment Effect in Pricing

Richard Thaler again (with help from Daniel Kahneman) gave us the idea of the *endowment effect*, and it helps us understand why people value some things more than others because they own them. In our context, think of the free trial; when you start using Canva, you understand how easy and revolutionary it actually is. So, after your trial was up, you didn't want to be downgraded to the basic version with limited benefits because it felt like something you owned was being taken away from you. So, opting for the subscription made a whole lot of sense.

Loyalty programs also work on a similar principle. Once I accumulate enough Marriott Bonvoy points,

I start becoming a bit too attached to them. Every time I look at the points balance, I see the promise of a new and "free" hotel stay. Hence, opting for a different chain of hotels means you don't get to add to something you already own and cherish - your relationship with Marriott.

Coupons and Vouchers

A few years ago, coupons meant something. It was almost like finding a ₹100 note in an old coat pocket. Now, coupons and vouchers are aplenty in the realm of eCommerce, whether you're buying biryani or binoculars. The way to make it work would be to enable your CLM systems to send each customer within the segment a unique coupon code that only they can redeem - "AY8UEO4O3892K" as a coupon code seems much more valuable than "WELCOME15".

Even for vouchers, if it's a beautiful piece of work - with your name engraved on it, with a unique code and persuasive (but never pushy) copy - customers will surely think twice before flinging it in the bin. Luxury brands and clubs often make such vouchers feel un-throwable, and hence the redemption rate for them improves.

Should You Be Sneaky in Pricing?

This is the part where we start evaluating the pros and cons of being transparent and fair while setting and communicating prices. Every supermarket, from D-Mart to Reliance Fresh to whatever is left of Big

Bazaar, talks about "everyday low pricing" or "*sabse saste din*" in some permutation or combination. That gives the customer a clear indication that you're claiming the best and fairest prices. Now imagine that you advertised as such, and the customer buys a month's worth of groceries and comes back to see that the prices on blinkit were actually cheaper. How trust-busting would that be?

Perceived unfairness is a sure-shot road to triggering outrage. People even rebelled when certain airlines introduced seat selection fees. Brands must be completely transparent in telling customers exactly what they're paying for. Opaque pricing models and hidden fees (particularly near checkout) lead to long-term brand erosion.

We all collectively hate surge pricing. Just because customers are willing to pay 1.5x the normal fare doesn't mean that cab aggregators should use that to their advantage and alienate the user with a lower willingness to pay. One can debate the capitalist angle in all this, but paying ₹800 for the same ride that was ₹400 some minutes ago isn't capitalism; it feels like daytime micro-robbery.

Marketers must use these pricing tricks to hack awareness and differentiate from competitors, but never for blatant manipulation. To be honest, while a brand may be able to score a short-term win, eventually, the rent will come due, and the brand would need to pay it with interest.

TURN INSIGHTS INTO ACTION

→ Position price on the axis of value rather than affordability. "Lowest insurance premium" vs "the best investment in your health" are two different approaches to similar communication

→ Prices that end with …99 or …95 work for lower and mid-priced products. Do the opposite for premium products and say ₹10,000 instead of ₹9,990.

→ Integrate comparison charts in your pricing table to play on reference pricing

→ Bundling products as combos with higher perceived value and lower total price (than the sum of its parts) can work wonders to drive more volume and increase gross margin

→ Use A/B testing to test the elasticity of your price for different consumer segments & regions by presenting different combinations of price and quantity.

→ Use campaigns like "back to school" or "summer vacation essentials" campaigns to trigger consumers' alignment to respective spending buckets in their mental accounting

→ Induce trial through "try-before-you-buy" campaigns, with generous giveaways to trigger both the compulsion of reciprocity as well as the endowment effect

→ Cashless payments via UPI, NFC or BNPL reduce the pain of paying further and enable larger ticket-size purchases

→ Be transparent in your pricing and display final prices (inclusive of shipping and taxes) so that the customer sees no surprises at checkout

→ During demand peaks (like rain), state the presence of surge pricing upfront, suggest alternatives to the customer, and send a push notification to inform the end of the surge pricing window - to maintain trust with the customer

8.

DECISION MAKING

The Interplay Between Emotion and Logic

Out of all kinds of consumers, Indians are perhaps the most complex. On the one hand, we act as expert accountants and do mental *hisaab* for every little expense. And on the other, we're splurging away our life savings on a single event - our child's wedding. There's a constant tug of war between logic and emotion in our lives that makes marketing an art for us.

But let's be clear: logic and emotion aren't enemies. They're more like *frenemies*. Logic likes to believe that it's running the show, carefully going over prices and features. But emotion often has the last laugh, nudging you towards those limited edition sneakers that may level up your social clout. The love-hate relationship between logic and emotion in our heads is what makes us rationally and irrationally human.

The Tug-of-War

Walking into a Reliance Fresh on a Sunday afternoon isn't much different from taking the Churchgate-Borivali fast at 7 PM on a weekday. Between the mayhem, you spot a new flavor of Maggi, *Korean*. You obviously love all things Korean, and you also love Maggi. Why would this not be your next favorite thing? You still pick up a 4 X Pack of the original Maggi because your emotional side can't bear the OG Maggi being tampered with. Your yummy companion on rainy evenings and late-night study sessions. You stick to your original, and it feels like love.

That's the nuance with which decision-making works in our brains. Technically, we should have just tried the new Korean Maggi, as it's not a life-changing decision. But emotion still got the better of us, and we stuck to what was familiar and loved. Marketers need to be able to understand and project this kind of behavior.

If you buy an EV, it has to appeal to logic and emotion at the same time. You need to navigate the specs, the range anxiety, and the total cost of ownership with your logical mind. But you also need to be able to tell yourself that you're doing your tiny bit to reduce the pollution levels in your city by driving an EV. A perfect pitch from a brand needs to balance both of these benefits for the customer.

Rational Decision-Making Processes

Rational thought often initiates our buying journey but then often gets trumped by emotional reasons. If you're buying insurance, then it's unlikely that you'll impulse-buy a 20-year term plan. You'll weigh options, compare prices, look at claim settlement ratios and whatever you can get your hands on. But in the end, you'll tell the relationship manager, "I'm going ahead with this because of your recommendation." The transparency, honesty, and potentially great after sales service from the rep helps you lean towards saying yes. The economic model of consumer decision-making, where the consumer is perfectly logical, doesn't practically hold ground.

How We Evaluate Features and Benefits

If you look at the smartphone space, it seems only one brand is talking the language of emotion, while all others appeal to your logic. Xiaomi, Vivo, Oppo, Samsung and RealMe - everyone's trying to outdo each other on specs. If someone comes up with a dual camera, someone has three and maybe four. If someone has a 5000 mAh battery, someone else's shouting about their 6000 mAh one. They know that we love comparing features. If you walk into a Croma, you'll have people flinging all kinds of specs at you: left, right and center. But the one that we all aspire to the most, doesn't talk about 1GB storage; they talk about 1000 songs in your pocket.

All D2C 'good-food' brands that sell clean whey protein, like Cosmix and The Whole Truth, know that our cognitive evaluation will consist of comparing ingredients in careful detail. We also want to put purity standards under the lens. That's where trust and credibility reign supreme for such brands since logical evaluation forms the bulk of the decision.

How We Assess and Perceive Value vs. Price

Nothing triggers our logical brains like a nice price analysis. Bargaining is a national sport in our country. There is no bad product; only a bad product at a bad price. At a lower price, the same product might be less bad. If you pay ₹500 for a coffee vs paying ₹250 vs paying ₹50 - your perception will dramatically change, even if it's the same cup of coffee in a blind test. Private brands are built on the principle of value for money - they'll give you a product that's "almost as good" as the market leader, but often at half the price. That changes the entire price-value equation for your logical mind, and that's why private labels are the highest gross margin products for a lot of retailers, online and offline.

Emotional Decision-Making Processes

Think of logic as something that brings the customer to the front door, and from there, emotion yells out loud, saying, "Come on in!" For most human beings, emotional decision-making is faster and more spontaneous, and it is likely to trump any logical thought.

Somatic Marker Hypothesis

This is super interesting research done by Antonio Damasio, who argued that emotions create feelings in our body called *"somatic markers"*, and these influence all subsequent decisions that we make. If you're anxious about something, and your heartbeat rises, that's a somatic marker, and it's likely to influence what you do next. Somatic markers help us make sense of the situation faster, see what it feels like, and quickly decide what to do next. This comes in handy, especially in complex situations.

If an investor is divided between selling or holding onto a stock, somatic markers can play a large role in their decision-making. All the world's financial indicators could suggest that they must hold it, but then, they get a strong feeling to sell it - since they remember the last time they held on during a similar trend, they lost a ton of money. Thus, the feeling in their gut triggered by the memory of their earlier financial loss sways them towards selling, even though the decision is strongly based on emotion rather than logic and evidence.

Emotional Contagion - how emotions truly go viral

This concept talks about how emotions spread from one person to another, influencing multiple decisions along the way. Such a convergence can happen from one individual to another or from one group to another, and it can even be observed in canines and birds. If you see too many people in an upscale mall wearing *Bluorng*, you'll search for the brand and would probably see what the fuss is all about. We've got an innate desire to conform. Everyone's ordering the same biryani? "Get one for me too".

When you're at a concert, and someone starts clapping, everyone else does, too. More so, if someone starts jumping and dancing with high energy, people around them experience a jolt of high energy and a desire to dance as well. This also often manifests in early-stage startups - when the founder walks into the office zapped and drained out of all energy, the same emotion rubs off on everyone in the office, and you can tangibly feel the ripple effect across the room.

Mood Congruence

This is just a fancy way of saying that people make decisions that match their current mood. You're feeling bummed? You'll order that banana pudding from Magnolia Bakery. Feeling pretty? You're more likely to spend on that Zara dress that you've eyed a couple of times before.

Beauty brands use this well. They position cosmetics as mood enhancers and self-care that you deserve after a long day's work. A red lipstick isn't just wax and pigment that makes your lips red; it's a 'confidence booster and a statement.' The logic behind buying that expensive lipstick becomes secondary to the emotional reward that you get out of it. So, when you're feeling confident and ready to slay the day, you wear red lipstick to make a statement and stand out unapologetically.

The Interplay Between Emotion and Logic

As we said earlier, emotion and logic aren't exactly enemies; they're more like frenemies. They don't compete - they kind of collaborate and make way for each other. Logic is the friend who makes Excel sheets before you leave for a trip, and emotion is the one who says, "Get in the car; we'll figure it out along the way."

You've been eyeing those Marshall speakers for a while because they just look so damn good! It feels like an emotional purchase where you want to be seen as someone who can afford a sleek, retro speaker that not only stands out from the dozen others aesthetically but also sounds amazing. But before you can drop ₹25,000 on a speaker, you need your logical voice to reassure you. It has a 5" subwoofer, 60W output, Bluetooth 5.2, and a one-year warranty. And! There's also a ₹1,000 cashback if you use your HDFC card. You can't miss this. This is your logic justifying what emotions have already decided you should buy.

This process is as irrational at times as it is interesting. Only campaigns which balance both these well (appealing to the heart as well as the head) will truly succeed in making customers open their wallets.

The Role of Heuristics in Decision-Making

Heuristics are mental shorts that enable you to make decisions quickly through fast responses that don't require too much thought and deliberation.

Availability Heuristic

We base our decisions on information that's readily available for us to recall. If it's fresh and available in our memory, then we're likely to buy the brand when the need arises.

If your child starts rejecting milk and needs a malt-based drink to make milk more palatable to them, then you instinctively reach out for Bournvita. That's the drink you grew up with, and those *tayyari jeet ki* ads were quite impressive. You won't necessarily launch a comparison exercise of Complan and Bournvita, figuring out each's nutritional value over the other. It's always been there, it's top of mind, so it's in your cart.

You need mosquito repellent stickers for your child before she goes to the playground to play. You've been hammered with advertising about Mamaearth being made *for mothers, by mothers* - using "toxin-free" ingredients. When the need arises, you open blinkit and see it on top. In 10 minutes or less, you're now a regular mamaearth customer.

Representativeness Heuristic

We often categorize products based on what we perceive as their similarities since doing this helps us decide quickly. We assume that something belongs to a certain category based on its similarity to the category's typical features.

Imagine you run into a strange-looking person at a coffee shop. He's got blue hair, oversized spectacles, and is sipping on a drip coffee while writing into a moleskine notebook with a pencil, occasionally staring into nothingness. Now, if you were to guess if this person was into advertising or stock trading, then most people would guess that he's an advertising professional, even though this might be untrue. That's because of the similarities his appearance has to what you perceive to be the archetype of a creative guy in advertising - and that's how you used the *representativeness heuristic* to slot them into that category without any substantive evidence.

Affect Heuristic

You're often very influenced by what you're currently feeling, and that trumps any logic in your decision-making. That's the *Affect heuristic*. Not very different from mood congruence.

Tom Ford makes fragrances for the confident and masculine man. Their packaging, brand design, and tonality project that its worn by the "alpha" male. And for men who feel that their masculinity is being threatened (which is, unfortunately, many men), they turn to overly masculine brands to help them feel empowered, not just well-groomed. There's a reason you have soft, rich boys driving around in mafia-spec G-wagons. Some controversially call it 'small D energy', which some may see as their short-term emasculation driving them to make outwardly masculine choices.

Manufacturing "Hot States"

Now that you know most of this, you can design experiences that gently push customers towards impulsive decisions - in other words, you can manufacture a *"hot state."* It's about creating a sense of excitement, urgency and probably even panic to ensure that customers decide super quickly in your favor. The customer would be experiencing a wave of intense emotions or cravings that could make them an easy target.

Restaurants and food courts are generally situated on the upper floors of malls. You start your window-shopping journey on the ground floor. You start shopping on the first floor (anchoring works here; shops on each upper floor get less & less premium and have cheaper rents and better deals). You find more deals on the second floor. By the time you're done shopping, you are ravenous. You could eat anything! After the effort and stress of trying on so many clothes and the decision fatigue, if someone puts a leafy salad in front of you, you're likely to punch them in the throat. You want something substantial. In your hot state, your craving for comfort food overpowers your commitment to choosing healthy food.

Nykaa's Pink Friday Sale creates such hot states by showing countdown timers and flashing "1 item left" over the buy now button. Driven by FOMO, customers purchase things they didn't even consider an hour ago. The manufactured hot state ensures that they skip the logical evaluation of whether they need 3 more body butters or not.

TURN INSIGHTS INTO ACTION

→ Multi-sensory ads (striking soundtrack, bright colors, strong hook) spark attention immediately and build quick emotional resonance before logic has a chance

→ Benefit comparisons and charts help customers rationalize features through logic, after emotions have done their job

→ Send rational follow-ups ("You saved ₹1500 through your Swiggy One membership in the past month) to reinforce that the customer's choice was smart one

→ Use personal stories in ads to trigger somatic markers; they add authenticity to your communication.

→ Optimize for top-of-mind keywords in common search queries to play on the availability heuristic

→ Align with your TG's familiar personas to create reliability and help customers use the representativeness heuristic

→ Feel-good words ("joy", "comfort", "earth") are more likely to get customers to unconsciously employ the affect heuristic and have a positive emotional response

→ Flash sales, countdown timers and limited stock are helpful in manufacturing a hot state and creating urgency where there is none

9.

HABITS & LOYALTY

*How Do We Get Addicted
to Some Brands?*

We are all creatures of habit. We don't even know it, but most of the time, brands are counting on us to be predictable. Some have become a part of our routines, on autopilot, almost like daily fixes. Whether it's starting your day with Nescafe or doom-scrolling through Instagram Reels while eating lunch at work, some brands and products have become deeply ingrained in our lives. This may not be because they're the best, but it's often because they're consistent. Consistency is the first step to addiction, and that's what marketers are looking for.

Take CRED, for instance. It started as a simple app to pay your credit card bills and get some coins while you're at it (the usability of those coins is still debatable). But over the last few years, they've slowly woven themselves into the fabric of the urban elite - what they call "India's most creditworthy customers." Once you're done paying your bills, you head to the rewards section; you sometimes check out the new drops in their store; you might even glance at CRED garage to check deals on car insurance or accessories. They've slowly made themselves a monthly habit for millions of well-heeled Indians. The app is now a weird kind of gamified rewards & shopping platform masquerading as a bill payment fintech app. And I am pretty sure that the monthly habit that they've managed to create is due to much more than Rahul Dravid pretending to be a road-rage maniac in Indira Nagar.

If we're talking about habits, then we surely have to talk about CULT.fit. They've put all their resources behind making fitness a daily ritual. Over time, this habit becomes so ingrained in the platform's power users that missing a CULT session could be akin to missing brushing their teeth. They've built a system of *triggers* (notifications and reminders), *rewards* (streaks) and *social pressure* (signing up for boxing class with friends). They've built a process that makes you want to keep coming back - even if you hate working out as much as I do.

Cue, Routine, Reward: The Habit Loop

How does this kind of addiction to brands and products even happen? In his book *The Power of Habit*, New York Times reporter Charles Duhigg laid out the loop in very simple terms: *Cue, routine, and reward*. Brands that crack this become a part of our lives without us even realising it.

What's the *cue* for Zomato? Hunger. What's the *routine*? Opening the app, scrolling through all the options and offers and finally ordering what you always do. The *reward*? Fast delivery to your doorstep with a side dish of guilt for eating too much "*bahar ka khana.*"

Brands that can create transparent and infinitely repeatable habit loops will bag those consumers for a long time. The *routine* eventually becomes a part of their lives, and the *reward* (whether it's pizza or a dopamine-fueled purchase) ensures that they keep coming back for more. They just have to make sure that the cue (this could be hunger or boredom) is a strong trigger for you to open their app.

Using Environmental Triggers to Reinforce Habits

Using triggers from the environment around a customer can really strengthen a habit. Starbucks tries to sell you a morning routine, which has their coffee. They sell the entire western habit of walking into a Starbucks before work and grabbing a takeaway of your caffeine fix on your way to tackle your 9 AM.

Starbucks is in the habit-creation business. The smell of those irresistible coffee beans as you walk by their coffee shop, the hum of the right music - that's the *cue*. The *routine* is to walk in, place your usual order, and see your name scribbled on the cup. The *reward* is to sip your yummy coffee on your way out. They want this multi-sensory experience to become less of a choice and more of a reflex.

Zepto also nails this. The *cue*? You ran out of onions. The *routine*? Open the app, add your usuals to the cart and checkout. The *reward*? Seeing your groceries arrive at the door in 10 minutes without having to haul yourself to haggle with the *sabziwala* or to carry multiple, heavy bags back from D-Mart. The sheer convenience of it all, along with the competitive pricing - makes Zepto (or blinkit or Instamart) a proper habit.

Can We Break and Replace Habits?

If habits are the holy grail for brands, then breaking old ones and replacing them with new ones where your brand is at the center - it's like discovering oil. But how do you get someone to switch to Jio after they've been loyal Airtel users for over a decade? Breaking a habit is tougher than pulling someone away from the last moments of a cliffhanger episode on Netflix.

Disrupting habits is hard. Jio didn't convince people to switch from Airtel by being a little better or a little cheaper. They changed the entire game by offering free unlimited data at a time when such a thing was unheard of. Suddenly, people were forced to question their existing loyalties. The cue had changed. The reward was relatively bigger, and that made people disrupt their deeply ingrained habits.

Reframing is an interesting method in which this can be done. CULT doesn't position itself as yet another gym. They position themselves as a lifestyle with a strong community element. They've reframed the experience of going to the gym from being a chore to a community-powered, streak-fed habit.

But if breaking habits was easy, then the world would be full of six-packs and ice baths. But it isn't. Disrupting and changing habits takes more than just offering an incrementally better product or service. It requires rethinking the customer's entire behavioral pattern.

Before Uber came into our lives, hailing a taxi (especially if you were in Bangalore or Delhi) was an exercise in patience. Uber didn't just replace traditional taxis in most cities - they fundamentally changed the habit. What we now take for granted was a revolutionary idea at launch. Booking a ride became a smooth, transparent and safe experience. No more haggling with drivers, being worried about them taking longer than the usual route; you could even see your tiny car zipping towards you. The entire experience was a step change over the legacy experience, and hence, it was able to conclusively disrupt our habits.

Can Brands Create New Habits?

Creating an altogether new habit requires brands to try and embed their products into customers' daily lives.

I'm a big fan of Sleepy Owl Coffee. Their cold brew packs or easy-to-make filter coffee are trying to slowly make coffee drinking a seamless and ritualistic habit. They've made sure they combine convenience with high-quality coffee to make sure that when you think of coffee at home - you grab your pack of Sleepy Owl Coffee as a part of your daily routine.

The creation of new habits requires the elimination of all kinds of friction in the customer's journey. Amazon Prime is arguably the world's largest subscription service. They didn't only sell you faster shipping but also bundled it with a bouquet of other services like video and music. And they made everything easier. Every time you now shop on Amazon as a Prime member, it feels like you're getting a deal, and things magically turn up at your doorstep, even if it's for a tub of peanut butter. The more you use Amazon Prime, the more embedded it becomes in your life.

Building a new habit requires offering something so convenient and valuable that it quickly seeps into the consumer's daily routine, and changing it feels like a task.

Is Brand Loyalty Even Real?

Well, that's a super debatable question. Is loyalty to your brand genuine or just a force of habit? Many founders like to parade some segments of their customer base as "loyal" when their repeated purchases are just a function of their inability (or disinterest) to break their routine, and the second a better alternative comes up, they will. Then, is it true loyalty? Do I really love Myntra, or is it just something that I am really used to?

Loyalty and habits are two sides of the same coin, but they are uniquely different. True brand loyalty is when a customer chooses your brand (*actively*) even when it's not the cheapest or most convenient option. They stick to you even when better challenger products are out there. Are people really loyal to Netflix? Or do they flirt with Prime Video on the side as well?

Brands often misinterpret habits and 'laziness to switch' as loyalty. I might keep buying the same brand of tea for decades, but is it because I am loyal or is it because it's decent and does the job? And I don't have a compelling enough reason to try any other brand of tea.

True brand loyalty is rare once you understand what it truly means. A loyal customer has a real, emotional connection with your brand beyond just the product. They become true advocates for your brand, not because it has the best features or pricing in the market, but because the brand is now a part of their identity.

Buying Saffola every time I need cooking oil is a *habitual purchase*; it's not because I am a die-hard fan of the brand or because it's the best cooking oil out there. But it's something I have always done - it requires no active thought or deliberation - it's an automatic choice.

On the other hand, *genuine brand commitment* can be seen in consumers of the brand The Whole Truth. Even when cheaper and more widely available options exist, you still wait for TWT protein and bars because the brand aligns with your values of trust, good food and transparency. It's not the cheapest out there by a mile, but you believe in what they stand for. That's genuine brand commitment.

The challenge for marketers is to switch habits into loyalty and true loyalty at that. Habits get you repeat purchases and high LTV, but genuine loyalty gets you that + advocates and lower CAC. The key is to build authentic relationships with customers and take the conversation beyond just the products to the values your brand stands for.

Awareness to Advocacy on the Loyalty Ladder

The loyalty ladder is when customers progress from being just aware of your brand to becoming true evangelists and advocates for your brand. But only if it were as easy as climbing an actual ladder - it's like navigating a minefield, where each step needs careful planning, deliberation and tight execution.

At the bottom of the ladder, you're a *prospect*, which means that you haven't yet purchased, but the brand could persuade you. You then become a *trialist*, a customer who has done business with the brand once. The next step up is to become a *supporter* when you like the brand and support it passively. And then comes the ultimate step on the ladder, when you actively start *recommending* the product to others (as an *evangelist*) and become an extended part of the brand's marketing team.

Once you've used Urban Company for sofa cleaning, chances are that you'll come back for more. Before you know it, a habit starts to take form. It's cheap and convenient, you don't have to haggle, and you know that you'll get top-quality cleaning done in no time. After repeated use, you start thinking that people who get their sofas cleaned from expensive local shops are doing it wrong; you start evangelizing Urban Company for sofa cleaning and may even start referring it to friends.

Advocacy will remain the holy grail of marketing. This is when consumers go out of their way to promote your products as the better alternative. Think of how Royal Enfield has made a legendary and irreverent brand that people love to associate themselves with. Supporters become advocates and evangelists, not because the brand pays them but because they genuinely care about the brand and its legacy.

The Psychology of Loyalty Programs

Loyalty programs are basically designed to trigger certain psychological impulses and make sure that you keep coming back to a brand. They make us feel rewarded for sticking with them, and loyal customers are statistically less likely to jump ship to a competitor.

CRED is built on the principle of *variable rewards*, where you don't know exactly what you'll get every time you play the casino game for rewards, and the mystery and dopamine make you keep coming back. Sometimes, you win something small like a cashback of ₹2, and sometimes, you win a voucher for a luxury hotel stay. But the anticipation keeps you hooked. The unpredictability is engaging.

When you collect a ton of reward points on your American Express card, the principle of *loss aversion* kicks in. You've been collecting those points for months now, and the idea of losing them makes you stick to the brand and continue spending with your AmEx instead of the three other credit cards that you have. You go out of your way to shop at stores where you can redeem your reward points because the thought of "wasting" them is intolerable. And that keeps you loyal.

Then, there are experiments like Tata Neu that integrate multiple brands under the Tata umbrella into one loyalty program. Tata Neu's core is the principle of *reciprocity* - the more you spend with Tata brands, the more you get rewarded. It feels like they're giving you something small back every time you shop with them, and that creates an invisible obligation to keep shopping with them. It's less about solitary transactions and more about deepening your relationship with them.

Can Gamified Loyalty Programs Increase Engagement and Retention?

In my opinion, gamification puts loyalty on steroids. It makes the entire process of earning and burning rewards feel like a game that you want to keep playing. Dunzo used to do this well. They would turn mundane deliveries into a challenge with a reward when you complete certain tasks. "Order 3 times in a week and unlock a special discount". These micro-challenges create an *engagement loop* that keeps customers hooked.

CRED does this with coins that are questionable in usability. The thrill of playing the casino with a chance to win big keeps you retained even when your coins may be worth less than dust.

Gamification makes it all about leveling up, completing challenges and streaks and getting that elusive dopamine hit from achieving something - even if it's something as simple as getting a free cup of coffee.

Loyalty Through Subscriptions

We'll have to talk about Amazon Prime again here because, let's face it - it's a masterclass on loyalty. The real genius behind the program is the *sunk cost bias*.

Once you've paid ₹1499 for the annual subscription, then every purchase seems like you're using that investment. You're rationalizing the cost and getting the most out of it, and Amazon wins every time you do.

The bundling of Prime Video, Prime Music, and a dozen other things makes it feel like you're getting a great deal, and somehow, loyalty turns into multi-attribute value. You're not just shopping; you're watching *Panchayat*, you're listening to Arijit Singh, and you're reading books on your phone. Thus, Amazon becomes an integral part of your digital consumption.

The subscription model, I am sure, doesn't guarantee Amazon revenue. However, it does turn occasional shoppers into loyal customers who eventually morph into power users of Amazon. Amazon Prime is the most beautiful example of how subscriptions can make loyalty turn from fleeting to permanent.

There's Always a Dark Side

Every marketing trick in the book has a dark side, and so do habits and loyalty. In their worst form, they are *exploitative, manipulative* and could potentially turn habits into dependence and, ultimately addictions.

Brands, often knowingly, nudge customers towards consumption patterns, which could be highly addictive. You know how minutes on Instagram Reels turn into hours. How one ping on WhatsApp can turn into hours of balancing multiple chat windows. But when does hyper-engagement cross the line into addiction?

Some research argues that this happens when the user is less in control of their behavior, and the habit is in more control of them. The habit turns into a reflex, which turns into a compulsion, which then turns into a necessity.

Take the addictive use of real money games - cricket betting apps or rummy ones. They've built habit loops that give an endless supply of dopamine to users with the possibility of a large financial reward. The *cue?* Cricket season, boredom over the weekend. The *routine?* Build a fantasy team, play a quick round of rummy. The *reward?* If you win, it's instant gratification - mentally and financially. If you don't, then there's always the lure of winning bigger the next time you play. It's an endless loop which often ends badly.

Real money gaming platforms are using the power of variable rewards where users keep risking their time and capital, often to their family's financial detriment. The unpredictability of rewards triggers the same notes in our brain as gambling does - where you keep going even if you lose, hoping that the next game will be the big one. What starts as a harmless game could spiral into a dangerous addiction where the lines between entertainment and financial foolishness are blurred. This is why the Indian government is spending more time and resources regulating apps like these and taxing them accordingly. The good thing is that most players are complying well.

Apps like these need to declare that they could potentially be habit-forming; otherwise, this becomes pureplay consumer exploitation. When habits like these can turn into addictions and the financial stakes become higher, the results can be catastrophic for consumers as well as for society.

145

TURN INSIGHTS INTO ACTION

→ Habit Loop

- Identify a frequent event or need state (like morning hunger, afternoon energy slump) to create the right cue and trigger a push notification

- Make the routine simple and integrateable in the consumer's life

- Offer instant gratification as rewards at relevant brand touchpoints to turn spontaneous purchases into habits

→ Habit Disruption

- Use trials and demos to get users to experience the new routine and evaluate vs. their existing habits

- Reframe the product in a new and unexpected way (cult.fit makes fitness a community experience rather than a chore)

- Demonstrate how your product substitutes the old habit, but also gives additional benefits over and above (e.g. swapping sugary colas for zero calorie alternatives)

→ Brand Loyalty

- Analyze CLM data to find the difference between true loyalty and habit-driven purchases by using engagement and repeat purchase data

- ◆ Help customers express and be rewarded for their advocacy via referral programs which give instant rewards

→ Loyalty Ladder

- ◆ Move customers from awareness to advocacy through sequential engagement, content and personalization

- ◆ Reward advocacy (in the form of referrals) and not only repeat purchase behavior

→ Loyalty Programs

- ◆ Incorporate small wins in terms of rewards that are immediate and frequent to keep them hooked

- ◆ Craft a tiering system and gamify it to reach higher levels

- ◆ Nudge how users may lose points or their access to member benefits if they don't engage with the program, thus triggering loss aversion

10.

PERSUASION

And Other Dark Arts

It's a Saturday afternoon, and you've decided to walk through that glitzy mall near your home. You have no clear shopping agenda, but to be really honest, neither did those dozens of people who walked out with shopping bags full of stuff they didn't plan to buy when they were going in.

You walk by the main atrium, and you're greeted by a cocktail of amazing scents: "the mall smell", fresh buns being baked at Cinnabon and the whiff of strong musky fragrances coming from the general area of a perfume kiosk with over-enthusiastic salesmen. If you look one level closer, this isn't a regular mall run; it's seeing persuasion out in the wild. Come with me as we walk through an imaginary mall and look at the seven wonders of Dr. Robert Cialdini's persuasion world.

Persuasion Is the Most Essential Marketing Skill

The mall isn't just a random collection of shops; it's a space carefully designed to make you bend your will. Every sight, smell and sound is designed to persuade - whether it's the beautiful window displays or the skilful store staff. Dr. Cialdini wrote two seminal books, "Influence" and "Pre-suasion", and this chapter is an homage to his work. It's as relevant for a B2B marketer as it is for someone looking to find a life partner.

Persuasion is a fundamental skill for a marketer. And if you've not come across the persuasion principles so far, fret not; we'll walk through the mall together and encounter each one of these principles. So, let's walk to our first store.

"I Love Free Stuff!" – Reciprocity

You've barely taken a few steps inside when, right outside Cococart, they're sampling some handmade chocolates. The store rep sweetly offers you the sampler, and you take one - it's nutty, creamy and just so delicious. Who could say no to a free chocolate? The moment your face lights up, the store rep asks you how it was and invites you inside the store. You now feel a strange nagging feeling - a sense of obligation. You need to buy something now. You can't just lie that the chocolate was bad.

That's the principle of *reciprocity*. If someone ever gives you something, you feel a strong urge to reciprocate and return the favor. Some brands will give you a big discount on the first order to acquire you as a new user and prompt you to return. SaaS companies do a free trial to trigger a symbolic sense of obligation to buy their paid plans since you enjoyed the full suite of features for a month. It works on most, I say most, because some of us are more easily persuaded than others.

Commitment and Consistency

We humans love to be consistent; we will do anything in our power to resist change. Once we've publicly committed to something, no matter how small, we feel the urge to remain consistent with that commitment.

We want to come across as reliable to others and honest to ourselves, too.

So when we see a standee for CULT's free demo yoga classes, we'll sign up, and then we'll rush into Decathlon to buy those yoga pants since you've got to look great while you slay the camel pose right? We'll consistently take action and make purchases which are consistent with this newfound *yogi* persona of ours. Brands push you to get your toe in the door, and they'll then make it a foot. Before you know it, you're fully inside, trying to remain consistent.

"If Everybody Jumps off a Cliff, Will You Too?" – Well, Yes.

Next up, you glance at a Xiaomi store that has 20+ smartphones on display. The walls are plastered with "India's #1 Smartphone Brand" and "Over 1 million units sold." And that's where you feel that so many people can't be wrong. That's the invisible pull of *social proof*. When you see a new agency's website, and they list the biggest brands out there as clients they've signed up already, you know that they aren't selling snake oil.

We've got a tendency to follow the herd, especially in cases when we want to protect our downside. When Bloom Hotels, a chain of budget hotels, tells you that "XX number of people checked-in last month", you're less likely to expect leaky taps and shady rooms. If a hotel property is labeled as a "best-seller", we know that so many people wouldn't have chosen wrong.

When you're shopping online, and they tell you that "68 people viewed this deal in the last hour", you feel a sense of urgency that might get you to rush to check out before any one of these imaginary people comes in and steals your deal from you. Social Proof tells us that when we're looking for signs of trust, we behave like sheep, and we assume that the largest flock knows the best pasture.

"Listen to the Expert, or the Celeb" – Authority

If you walk into any supermarket at the mall and you come across Navratna Oil, you wonder why Amitabh Bachchan still endorses this brand and if it works. Big B sells trust, and brands rush to grab a piece to rub onto themselves. Navratna oil positions itself as the ultimate stress reliever, and to their target audience, if Mr. Bachchan says it works, they're convinced. That's the principle of *authority* in action.

Marketers love celebrity endorsements. Some of us label it as a lazy strategy, while many others know that it's the quickest path to hack awareness and to cement the right brand associations, borrowing from the celeb's brand equity.

We love seeing authentic dentists in Sensodyne ads because that lab coat and the interview-style ad make it authentic as well as authoritative. The science looks probably legit, but using authority figures in their communications makes it even more believable.

"I Like You, So I'll Buy From You" – Liking

Back to our mall stroll, we walk into the Chumbak store and are greeted by a charming salesperson helping us pick out the nicest cushions and tote bags. She's funny, relatable, not pushy, at all. Somehow, she seems genuinely interested in what you like and what part of your home the cushion is for. She seems nice, and you feel more obligated to buy and don't want to walk out empty-handed from the store now that you've had a rather pleasant conversation with the knowledgeable salesperson. You may not need all 6 of the cushions you ended up buying, but we love to buy from people we genuinely like.

That's the power of the *liking* principle. Tupperware and Avon were built on the fundamental insight that people may not need another set of plastic containers or night creams, but when recommended by a person they like, they're way more likely to buy. Personal relationships continue to be the highest leverage point for brands like these, and they use it well.

"Catch Me If You Can" – Scarcity

You're now in the Puma store trying on the new RS-X sneakers, which you think look fire. There's a 20% discount too! It's your lucky day. You ask the store rep to bring it in your size, and he says that the RS-X stock in the UK-10 size has been finished. You shrug your shoulders and start looking at other sneakers, which now look like consolation prizes to you. Then suddenly, the store rep comes back with a box in hand and says, "Sorry, Sir, there was one pair left somewhere; it probably had your name on it." You sprint to the cash counter and bill it before he can say another word. You loved the sneakers, but the fact that they were scarce and not available made you desire them even more.

When OnePlus launched their first phone, the OnePlus One, they famously used an invite system without which you couldn't buy the phone. That was probably one of the best uses of the *scarcity* principle in the smartphone segment ever. People were selling invites on eBay, and many friendships were ruined when buyers gave out their invites to some friends when others missed out. That launch remains among the best examples of the scarcity principle I've ever seen.

The Game of Pre-suasion

After a quick stop at the washroom, you're ready to walk to the other side of the mall. The air still has a whiff of potential purchases in it, and you're ready to whip out your credit card like a modern-day cowboy in a gunfight. As you walk ahead, you encounter stuff you'll read in Cialdini's second major book, "Pre-suasion", and we'll uncover it during our stroll ahead.

Attention

We've spoken about this in detail in the chapter on attention, but the way Dr. Cialdini talks about this is rather nuanced. Attention works on three axes: *sex, danger and novelty*. You see the grand facade of the Zara store. It's designed to grab attention, tease the hero styles of the season and make you stop and decide to walk in to check the clothes out. There's a massive poster of a model in monochrome that you can see as you walk in, with provocative angles and sultry looks.

Sex is one of the most potent attention-grabbers. It's deployed into our biology. The sexy and sultry vibe of the imagery around the store is meant to create a sense of arousal, allure and aspiration. If you see a confident and sexy model wearing that trench coat, you're likely to try it on yourself.

But it's not only about sex. Zara's strategy, beyond their supply chain prowess, works on *novelty*. They have one of the fastest merchandise change-over cycles in the industry. You walk in often to check out the newer cuts, the latest textures, and patterns which are just off the runway. Novelty catches our attention since we're always on the lookout for things that would make us stand out and get noticed, particularly in fashion.

Context

Everyone should walk into a Tiffany and Co. store just once to experience the level of *retail* that is performed in front of you. Even before you step inside, you can see the typical Tiffany Blue (#81D8D0), which gives you a feeling of exclusivity and timeless elegance. You've seen the ads on Instagram, and you've seen the brand in pop culture. You walk into the store, and it smells divine. There's soft jazz playing in the background. The lighting is just dim enough to add a touch of mystique and just perfectly focused on pieces they want you to notice first.

All of this is context in action. Even before you could set your eyes on the first product or even be greeted by the store reps, Tiffany had already played their psychological games.

The game had already been set up even before the store rep greeted you in refined language and slipped in compliments for what you're already wearing. None of this is accidental. The theater of retail is designed to build the right context before the ask can be made.

Unity

Royal Enfield sells their merchandise mostly in their bike showrooms, but now they've started doing exclusively-merchandise outlets as well. Let's talk about their clothes - what do they sell? Rugged aesthetic, vintage biking-culture-inspired apparel. In almost all their communication, you can see the sense of "*unity*" - Royal Enfield riders helping other riders stuck on the road to Leh. The brand's not only about its history; it's also about inviting people to the tribe. Royal Enfield is about unity, adventure, and freedom, and that is reflected in all the choices they make inside their store. Humans have an inherent need to conform and feel that they're a part of something bigger than themselves, and Royal Enfield plays on this consistently.

So, by the time you exit the mall, you've experienced enough persuasion (and pre-suasion) in action. The next time you go to a mall, look out for these tactics before they get the better of you. Even if you spot them, they might.

TURN INSIGHTS INTO ACTION

→ Reciprocity - use surprise freebies, early access deals to your loyal customers and "thank you" discount codes to thank people for signing up

→ Commitment & Consistency - Start with a "yes" question like "Is your rising electricity bill bothering you?" and use a foot-in-the-door technique to get customers to move up your tiered loyalty ladder

→ Social Proof - real-time updates like "4 people bought this in the last hour" help in creating social proof. Liberally use "best-sellers" and "tribe favorites" tags to help people quickly discover and build trust.

→ Authority - Put authoritative logos and certifications up front (FDA approval, ISI etc.) and have known experts create content reviewing your brand

→ Liking - Do a behind-the-scenes "meet the team" campaign for your brand; people love it when they know that they're buying from a small business with real humans

→ Scarcity - "deal ends in XX Minutes" countdown timers still work, as do "low stock" alerts

→ Attention - use motion graphics wherever possible to draw instant attention and use contrasting colors for CTAs

➜ Context - curate the music, mood and overall look and feel of your retail environment in such a way that half the sale is done before the customer picks up any product. There's tons of advanced research on this that you can refer to.

➜ Unity - Bring out the feeling of community and camaraderie, which taps on your customers' FOMO of being a part of something larger and more bragworthy

11.

NEUROMARKETING

Brain Meets Branding

Neuromarketing is the lovechild of neuroscience, psychology and marketing. Think of it as a world where Freud meets Facebook ads, and Pavlov's dogs are no longer drooling, but they're figuring out which coloured packaging makes consumers salivate the most. It's a field where you stop *asking* consumers what they think and start figuring out what they *really* think by looking directly inside their brains. If you've done a focus group where half the participants are zoned out, you know the frustration. Neuromarketing lets you cut through the bullshit and get straight to the answers you want.

Neuromarketing has long been some marketers' secret weapon. Using it, you can tap into the subconscious and look at hidden desires by looking at parts of the brain that we don't yet fully understand - like Sherlock Holmes assisting you in figuring out why you can't resist the second pair of red heels. Neuromarketing works all around us - from supermarket shelves to annoying push notifications. Nothing is an accident. All these tactics are as precise as brain surgery, carefully designed for us to do what we do without us even knowing it.

I am a Spotify loyalist. But I often wonder how exactly they know what mood and genre to suggest to me and how to slip in ads at exactly the right point; that annoys me enough to buy premium but not as much to close the app. They'll craft the perfect playlist for my Monday blues, and just when I'm really enjoying it, they'll slip in the "premium for ₹99 a month" pitch, working masterfully at my dopamine circuits.

Old School Marketing Research to New Age Neuromarketing

Traditional marketing research is much like a polite conversation over tea. As a management trainee, I had the fortune (or misfortune) of being a part of many focus groups - which are basically a series of unending "How did that make you feel?" questions. But over the years, you develop the understanding that what consumers *think, say, feel and do* - are often four different things.

Humans overthink, over-analyse, lie - especially in social situations like focus group discussions where we want to look acceptable in front of strangers. Sometimes, we just may not know how to articulate our true feelings about something. Other times, we just don't want to. In traditional marketing research, marketers are left piecing together a jigsaw puzzle with many missing pieces.

Frito-Lay famously used Neuromarketing to improve its packaging design. They switched their bright and shiny packaging for a matte bag with healthier ingredients on display as they found out that women are more likely than men to experience guilt while binging on salty snacks. And, of course, sales improved. In traditional marketing research, who would have even told them that their packaging made them feel more guilty? But Neuromarketing cut through all the posturing and brought them to the root cause.

Meet Your Brain

Let's try and understand the place where all the magic happens. If you wondered why you bought that extra-large tub of popcorn instead of the large one or bought the new iPhone even when your old one worked just fine, blame your *limbic system, prefrontal cortex* and *amygdala*. Consider these as the holy trinity of consumer behavior.

The *limbic system* is like your emotional powerhouse. It's the part that lights up when you see a cute baby, an emotional ad or a limited-time offer. It works on responses that are instinctual in nature - where you don't think much, just feel. If you can trigger the limbic system as a marketer, then you've pretty much got their hands reaching for their credit cards.

The *prefrontal cortex* is where decision-making takes place. Think of it as the rational side of your brain, where you weigh options and think about the long-term implications of your decisions. This is the part that keeps the limbic system in check. When you're considering buying that new SUV, this is the part that does all the evaluation (financial, emotional, social).

Finally, there's the *amygdala*. This is the primal fear center. If you really want to use this part well, you need to harness the power of anxiety to your advantage. You could trigger urgency ("only 1 item left") or pure

FOMO; the amygdala is the part that tells you to act since it believes that if you don't buy it now, you'll keep regretting it.

Neurotransmitters and Decision-Making

Meet your best friend and enemy - *dopamine*. You may know it as the brain's "feel good" chemical. It's what makes you feel great when India wins a T20 game, when you eat the yummiest gelato and, of course, when you have something you want to buy and have had your eye on for a while. Dopamine is the most important one for marketers to understand since it fuels *anticipation*. When you think you're about to get a reward (like a new pair of headphones, a killer deal on a dress, or the thrill of unboxing a new pair of shoes), dopamine rushes to flood your brain. This is where brands design their entire strategy around triggering these tiny doses of dopamine.

When you pay a bill on CRED, you collect coins. And then you burn those coins to potentially win a jackpot. This is what triggers the release of dopamine, not because the reward is great (which in most cases isn't) but because of the sheer anticipation of getting something unknown. This dopamine rush makes you come again next month after having paid your credit card bills, no matter how annoying you think their app animations are.

But dopamine isn't the only player in this game. There's *serotonin*, the one which stabilizes your mood. And then there's *oxytocin*, which is often called the bonding hormone. Brands that make you feel like you're a part of a community, tap into these chemicals. Think about how Nike does it. They don't position themselves as a running shoe brand; they talk about the feeling of achievement, belonging and becoming the best version of yourself. That's serotonin and oxytocin working together to make you feel that you're a part of *something bigger than yourself*, even though you're just buying a pair of shoes to run in.

How Is Neuromarketing Done?

Let's talk about the gadgets and techniques neuromarketers use. It's quite science fiction-ish, but I'm sure you'll love going down this rabbit hole. Marketers now have access to tools that can truly look inside their consumers' brains, understand their eye movements and monitor their physiological responses to anything you put in front of them - your product or your ad.

fMRI (Functional Magnetic Resonance Imaging) is the one that's used most often. It basically puts consumers inside a big MRI machine and sees which part of their brain lights up when we show them things. This helps marketers understand how consumers react emotionally and rationally to their products, ads, designs, or anything. Coca Cola is known to have used this to understand reactions to different types of can designs.

EEG (Electroencephalogram) measures waves emanating from the brain. It captures how engaged a consumer is when they're looking at your stuff. Are they interested, or did they zone out in seconds (or less)? Many brands spend a fortune on ATL advertising, and doing an EEG study would tell them if the hook into their ad is working or tanking.

Eye-Tracking or GSR (galvanic skin response) is more easily doable without as many expensive machines. *Eye-tracking* looks at where exactly on a landing page your eyes moved and stopped. Did you notice the CTA button? *GSR* measures physiological responses like sweating to see if you are emotionally excited about seeing the stimuli. Both of them present the truth without the filtration applied by speech.

Applications of Neuromarketing

Now that we've understood the tools used, let's try to see how brands use them practically. Netflix uses a ton of A/B testing to decide which thumbnail for a movie will get the maximum CTR. However, they don't only rely on the CTR metric; they liberally use eye-tracking to see which elements on the thumbnail worked and which didn't. Was it the image, the font, the color scheme or something else? Netflix optimizes and serves users with the ones that are known to get the maximum number of clicks from watchers.

Apple designs its stores (on the back of eye-tracking neuro data) in such a way that everything feels sleek, at ease and triggers a sense of aspiration. They used Neuromarketing to understand that clean lines, open and well-lit spaces, and minimalist displays create a sense of calm at a deep level, which comes in handy when you're overspending on that top-spec Macbook Pro.

Cadbury has used Neuromarketing to optimize its packaging - every little detail: color, texture, etc. They understand that consumers associate certain colors and packaging materials as more premium than others, and they've used that to their advantage.

Can Neuromarketing Uncover Hidden Consumer Desires?

Neuromarketing can potentially not only tell us what consumers want but also tell us what they *don't even know* that they want. People may say that they bought a brand for a certain reason, even though their brains might be telling a completely *different* story. The hidden reasons behind what we *do* and what we *feel* are buried deep into our subconscious, and Neuromarketing can possibly dig them up.

You might be thinking that you're ordering *tres leches* from Magnolia Bakery because you're hungry and craving something sweet, but Neuromarketing will show that you're *craving comfort* and a hug. And the *tres leches* is the closest thing to it, within reach. Understanding customers through neuromarketing helps us uncover deeper emotions like these, and thus, marketers can tap into triggers that customers didn't know they even had.

Ads may follow you around the internet due to cookies - but they connect with you at a deep emotional level because they've been neurologically toughened.

Neuromarketing helps iterate each content piece till it becomes super efficient in getting the desired response. Nike ads show athletes and everyday people pushing their limits, and these visuals trigger the brain's emotional centers, which deal with ambition and chasing goals. It feeds into our innermost desire to achieve, improve and ultimately be the best version of ourselves. Neuromarketing helps fine-tune this emotional tug-of-war to make sure it hits the right notes.

Ethical Considerations in Neuromarketing

Neuromarketing, while revolutionary, has triggered its own set of debates. Just because we can look inside someone's brain doesn't mean that we *should*. There is a fine line between influencing consumer behavior and blatant manipulation.

At the very core, this discipline is about understanding the natural responses of the human brain to marketing stimuli. It helps us understand what people actually feel behind the cloak of what they explicitly say. But it also unearths people's most vulnerable feelings and emotions for companies to profit from, and therein lies the problem. Once this gets into areas of addiction, mental health, etc., this is where the ethics become even murkier.

Apps use neuroscience to understand their users' dopamine-triggering behaviors to make them engaged and buy for longer than they would have originally wanted to. The data helps us create rewards which further push customers into an endless loop that's hard to consciously break. While this may boost profits, unhealthy usage of certain products and brands comes with its own costs.

This raises some critical questions: Is Neuromarketing designed to serve customers or deviously make them buy more? And not everyone is as transparent about using these tools as they should be. Consumers fundamentally should know when and how they're being played. So, is Neuromarketing helping or adding to the problem?

I agree that Neuromarketing is a powerful tool when it is in the hands of the right marketers. It will surely help us design and offer better products and solve consumer problems better. But only if used *responsibly*. Brands need to be more transparent and ethical and declare the use of such techniques since they can have a big impact on consumer habits and lives overall. Consumer trust, once lost, is impossible to gain back. Only marketers who truly respect the autonomy of consumers will be able to create long-term and symbiotic relationships, not those who manipulate them.

12.

THE PSYCHOLOGY OF AI

*It Hasn't Killed Us Yet,
Thankfully.*

Every conclave or mainstream interview of any CMO in this country has one *ghissa-pita* question: "How do you think AI will change things?" I am honestly fed up with the mediocre questions asked by advertising and marketing beat journalists. And even more fed up with the templatized and rehearsed answers given by our top CMOs. We really need to move beyond the fact that AI is now the shiny new toy in any marketer's toolkit. We shouldn't be debating if AI will take marketer or agency jobs; we should be deciding how best to ride this wave that's unlikely to ebb any time soon.

Probably a decade ago, AI was kind of a sci-fi concept where robots were going to basically rise and kill us. Fast forward to today, it hasn't killed us (at least at the time of writing this), but it somehow permeated every part of our lives - from our Netflix recommendations to the dark store near our home that knows when to re-stock atta before you expect another bag to reach your doorstep in ten minutes. For marketers, I think that AI is the biggest thing that has happened to our field since television. It's like having a psychic who knows your customer better than you, can do a ton of work for you intelligently and also make all your communication more timely and relevant.

However, the real magic is not how AI helps in a predictive capacity but how it potentially can turn old, hard training data into real emotional resonance with customers. AI-driven marketing can dissect every little action and breadcrumb left by the customer on the internet and figure out the most well-crafted message to serve them at the most suitable time and platform. Marketing that uses AI well is personalized, fast, predictive, and eerily accurate.

How Consumers Perceive and Interact with AI

Not all customers are uniformly excited and comfortable with AI. If you've ever used the self-checkout lane in a supermarket abroad, then you know the feeling. You're convinced that it's useful, but it's slightly *intimidating*.

How customers perceive AI in marketing is a function of how seamlessly it plugs itself into the customer journey. I love Amazon's AI-driven product recommendations. If Amazon starts recommending the perfect coffee maker because you just bought some expensive coffee beans last week, then it makes sense. But the moment it starts pushing swimming gear to you because you browsed some towels yesterday - then it quickly gets into creepy territory.

And then there are the AI chatbots - the first responders who sound like emotionless machines on customer service chats. We've all lost our temper when our Swiggy or Zomato delivery took longer than expected. In those moments, we found ourselves chatting with what was clearly an AI, missing the good old days when we could yell at a human customer service representative. Back then, we could pretend that the delayed order had embarrassed us in front of our friends and demand compensation. With AI chatbots, you're often stuck in a loop of misunderstandings and templatized hollow responses.

Why Do Some People Adopt AI Faster Than Others?

One wonders why some adopt AI in their lives quicker than others and what the role of cognitive psychology is in this. Of course, our brain loves anything that makes life easier. If the AI helps us find the best route to Nandi Hills or suggests a re-order of toothpaste via Alexa - it's one less thing that we need to remember and do. And we love things that make our lives easier.

However, we humans have a deep-seated disdain for anything making us perceive that we're losing our autonomy and control. When AI stops only *suggesting* and starts making automated *decisions* for us, that's when we could feel that we're giving up more decision-making power than we would like. It's the same feeling that you get when YouTube nails your suggested videos, but one day, you open your home feed and see that YouTube probably knows you better than your partner. The trick must be to make AI feel like a helpful assistant and not a creepy stalker.

What Kind of Emotional Responses Do We Have to AI?

The range of emotions that we've started experiencing with AI is quite dazzling. Some are excited, others are confused, some are anxious, and some are downright dismissive. Though they're not as popular in India yet, smart fridges are an interesting case study to understand this. A decent smart fridge is capable of understanding that you're low on milk and can go ahead and order it for you. To some, this outcome is like living in the future already, and to some, it's apocalyptic.

To be honest, for most, AI still triggers fear and anxiety. And it's not about AI snatching our jobs from us, but it's about the unease of being observed, evaluated and manipulated by an algorithm. The collection of data - everything from our sleep patterns to shopping ones - feels like a reenactment of the *Truman Show*, where everything that you do is recorded, analyzed and then used back to sell more stuff to you. The idea of AI being more competent at many things we do at work is also unsettling to many.

What Builds or Erodes Trust in AI?

The argument of trust somehow has made its way to the center of the AI debate. Humans trust humans (not always, but often). But trusting AI - that's a leap of faith. How do you sit in a car that uses *Tesla's autopilot*? Its novelty value is understandable - you are thrilled and excited to see how it works the first time. But can you integrate it into your life fully yet? The moment there's news of an autopilot accident, trust erodes immediately. It's like you were already suspicious of it, the news just gave you ammunition to never use it. Taking it a step further, would you sit inside a *Tesla Robotaxi* with nobody in it?

People are known to be far more forgiving of AI whenever companies are *transparent* about it. When they feel that they can control it, and also shut it. They can choose how it engages with them and what kind of data of theirs gets shared to sharpen the AI's responses. It's all about feeling that AI is on their side and not out to creep them out or make them feel like an inferior being.

Personalized Marketing: The Balance Between Relevance and Creepiness

At the very fundamental level, personalized marketing should work for most of us as we have a basic human flaw: *we want to feel special.* Every time you receive something that's meant just for you and not for CustomerID XXXXX, you feel something stroking your ego a bit. And when an algorithm curates an irresistible feed, you feel that "they get me."

Any kind of personalization creates a vague sense of *ownership*. "This is mine, it's for me" - whether it's your Netflix recommendations or a look curated for you. Even though you know that it's an AI doing it, on some level, you don't feel like a faceless customer; you're someone of value who matters to the brand. Their ability to personalize what you'd like reflects your time with them. That is a loyalty-triggering loop.

But, it works till a point. You want to be aware of how your data is being used to feed these recommendations back to you. You want to be able to switch it off if you want to. It should feel like service, not surveillance.

How Does Amazon Do This Well?

Arguably, no company on earth knows your shopping habits better than Amazon. Their systems don't just predict what you'll buy next; they'll also suggest it. Whether it's your browsing or searching history, device type, session time and duration, location - everything is feeding the beast to come up with irresistible recommendations in the form of "Customers who bought this, also bought…"

Amazon's AI-powered systems also know when and how to stock warehouses in anticipation of what you'll buy next. There's less publicly available information about this, but it's alleged that they can also adjust real-time prices with their algorithms based on anticipated demand. That's what keeps them at the top of the global eCommerce game, at least for now.

What one customer may perceive as helpfulness and customer understanding, others will see as manipulation. And that's where the debate's interesting.

Perception of and Engagement with AI-Generated Content

AI is even generating ad films now, and it's so far being met with mixed reactions. Some love the speed and low-cost nature of doing marketing at scale, while others lament the lack of soul and human touch. If an image clearly looks AI-generated, you're far more likely to distrust the brand, saying, "A person didn't shoot this; a computer spat it out." That erodes trust and engagement and makes the pursuit of efficiency through AI altogether futile.

In current form, most people find AI-generated videos off-putting; maybe that'll change in a few months, looking at the speed at which these things are improving. Maybe at that point, we'll have a fresh set of concerns to worry about.

Manipulation, Deception, and Missing Ethics in AI Use

We've all felt manipulated or thrown off by some kind of AI. That feeling of being creeped out raises questions about the ethics of how we're using AI, particularly in marketing.

AI can be used to deceive - it could generate deepfakes, create misleading and hallucinatory product recommendations and swiftly change pricing, depending on how much you're willing to pay. We've all tried this - two phones at the same location often see different prices for the same destination in different cab aggregator apps. This kind of AI-driven price optimization is unimaginable in the real world. Imagine if the shopkeeper changed the price tag of the dress, looking at the handbag you were carrying.

AI's ability to auto-generate customer service responses also blurs the line between real conversation and what feels like deception. Consumers are starting to question whether their experiences are real, which feels like a slippery slope for any brand.

AI Influencers: Why Haven't They Taken Off?

A couple of years ago, AI influencers felt like the next big thing. Turns out, we don't care.

Despite all their advanced graphics and human-mimicking personas - all AI influencers lack one crucial thing: *authenticity*. Lil Miquela, one of the best-known AI influencers, may have tons of followers, but she is still devoid of the messy, erratic and genuine content that makes many other influencers feel human and relatable.

Now that the novelty factor has worn off, consumers can spot an AI influencer from a mile away, and they're not buying anything from her. Not yet. We still need real humans with backstories and real emotions. We want to see influencers with good hair days and (very) bad hair days. And that's something AI cannot replicate, yet.

I don't think AI influencers will be a total failure in the future, though. They will still have uses in niche areas like high fashion or high-tech gadgets if done right. But the *"done right"* bit seems to remain a challenge currently.

We Don't Like AI That's Too Human-Like

Research suggests that if AI is too human-like, we get really uncomfortable. This is the strange point at which AI is very human-like but not exactly human, so we feel a strong repulsion towards it. It's especially unsettling when you see a machine mimicking human behavior with warmth, humor, intuition and authentic imperfection.

Voice-based assistants like Siri and Alexa work because they never pretend to be human. They're clearly machines that can play *Despacito* for you. But, if and when they try to be too friendly or too human, you'll be creeped out and unplug it. We can tolerate AI chatbots in customer service chats, but if we notice the AI using quirks and emotions that it shouldn't display that's when the conversation takes a sharp turn.

The future of AI will need to navigate this. Future applications need to ensure that we don't try to pass it off as human and be honest about what it actually is.

The Balancing Act

The challenge for marketers remains to use the power of AI in their marketing without crossing into territory that's unethical or uncomfortable. AI will continue to get better, and consumer expectations will also heighten. Brands need to ensure that there is a fine balance between personalization and privacy, helpfulness and overreach.

In the end, AI would never be about replacing humans in marketing or the human element. It's about enhancing customer experiences in a way that our ability to understand, empathize, and serve becomes exponentially better. No matter how well AI evolves from here, the human touch will always make all the difference.

EPILOGUE

The Rabbit Hole Goes Deep –
Deeper Than Your Wallet

You brave, brave person - here you are! At the finish line of this journey of psychological nudges and magic tricks that would make PC Sorcar proud. We've talked about why we buy overpriced cappuccinos, why loyalty points sometimes feel like shackles rather than rewards, and why sometimes "curated offers" seem like they were made just for you, even though that email went to numerous others.

After all of this reading, you may be wondering, "But what's *marketing* really about?"

Is it about making people feel good while they hand over their money? Or, as we said earlier, is it about not only selling a *product* but also *feeling*? A feeling that, for a moment, would make life seem slightly better. The best marketers tell us that it has always been about one thing - making people feel that they're buying into something that would make them a better version of themselves. Even if it's deodorant.

But It's Always a Fine Line

Look at marketing like you look at your uncle on the paternal side. He's kind of funny and charming, but sometimes he's a bit weird. He tells you a ton of stories about when he was young, but you're not sure how many you should believe in. Or the old classmate who DMs you out of the blue and asks you to meet to show you something that's making him money. You think, "Is he going to sell me something, some network marketing scheme?". Mostly not, but sometimes yes.

But that's the beauty of marketing. It's a strange blend of truth, half-truths, some magic and a whole lot of ridiculousness. The goal is never to lie or hard sell outright but to be compelling and interesting enough to be believable.

It's about making the banal into something special. Like taking a bottle of carbonated sugar water and making you feel that it'll "open happiness" for you. Marketing's real genius lies in its ability to make you think that spending ₹24,990 on AirPods Pro is actually an investment into your productivity and mindfulness practice.

Somehow, We Love Being Nudged

I think we can safely conclude by now that humans are essentially weird. We strangely like being sold to, sometimes. We like being persuaded, wooed and courted. But only as long as we feel that we're the ones in control. When someone says, "no pressure, but you should *totally* try this" - you know that there's pressure, but you've already mentally decided to give it a shot. Because who wants to miss out, right?

That's the reason marketing works. It's never about hard coercion, but it's about a soft, gentle nudge that pushes you just over the fence. You want a new ergonomic chair to sit in your home work-desk, and a voice in your head whispers to you saying "Go ahead, you deserve it man." It's an investment in your posture and productivity. Who can argue with that? The chair brand didn't sell you the product; they sold you a story of comfort and long hours of deep work.

We're all in on the joke. We know that "Up to 80% off" means nothing special, and "limited stock" may be just another tactic. But we'll still walk into the store and click that banner on our screens. We'll play along. We know that the "new and improved formula" on the packaging is the same old thing. We believe in these claims as we believe in Santa Claus - we know it isn't real, but we'll still play along.

We're Moths Sometimes

And we're drawn to the flames of discounts. If anything says "FLAT 60% off", we'll always look. Often if we don't even have a use for it. It's not as much about the product as it is about the feeling of victory and the rush you get from stealing a deal. It's a strange belief of "beating the system." When your partner excitedly comes to you and shows you the new dress she got from Myntra and asks you, "Guess how much it was for and how much I got it for?" - she's expecting you to guess that she practically stole this deal and got it before someone else could. It's like finding two packets of masala in your Maggi - it's a small win, but often feels monumental.

When you snatch a BOGO offer, you may not have needed two tubs of strawberry ice cream, but they made their way to your freezer somehow. That's the genius of it all. You didn't want two; you probably wanted a different brand altogether. But you walked out with two and a sense of achievement.

We're the Sum of Our Minor Existential Crises

If there's one thing that you take away from this book, it should be this - every purchase is, in some way, a minor existential crisis. When I buy a black goth T-shirt, it's a bid to look cooler (and more mysterious?). Sometimes it's just a cry for help. If I show up to work in that goth tee, then I am making a conscious choice to be *that* person. I am not the blue shirt and khaki trouser robot, but I am someone who doesn't care about how he turns up as long as he likes what he wears. And that's the identity that I am projecting and reinforcing with my unfortunate sartorial choice.

And yet, every morning, we're overwhelmed by the same choice. We stand in front of our wardrobes and become curious cases of choice overload. Every day. Which one would make me look slimmer if I'm feeling bloated? Which one would make me look like Ryan Gosling (*if you find a t-shirt that does this, please email the author*). Every choice is a vote for the person you want the world to see you as. And that's the origin of all our existential crises.

Hope, Guilt and FOMO

You know by now that all purchases need to hit one of these three buttons. You probably saw someone's post on LinkedIn and FOMOed into buying this book, with the HOPE that you'll read something useful (*and I hope it has delivered on that promise*). But whether we're buying educational toys for our toddlers or signing up for a

Pilates class - marketers continue to play us better than our therapists.

Hope is the easier one to sell. Your air fryer was hope. Hope of a healthier *you* who avoids non-essential fats like the plague. It'll be the same hope that will make you buy a CULT membership in early January. Hope powers the beauty industry too. "This will be the year when I finally learn to play the piano" - you'll say that and fizzle out before January ends.

Guilt is a close second, to be honest. Hamleys is built on the guilt of busy parents who see Hamleys at the airport and take a toy back for their child to mildly compensate for the time they spent away. It's the guilt that prevents you from un-selecting the "Donate ₹2 to charity" option at check-out. As a marketer, you're selling absolution.

And finally, there's FOMO. We've discussed its power in this book. And you should be able to go back and think "How can I trigger my target audience's FOMO?" FOMO makes even the most skeptical of us cave in and queue up for a ticket to a Coldplay concert. Even though Puritans will question us about how many songs of theirs have we heard.

Marketing Is a Love Letter to Our Flaws

I've realized that marketing, at its core, is a celebration of our imperfections. It understands that we are fundamentally flawed, sometimes forgetful and often lazy. But it doesn't judge us. It just uses those impulses to give us what we want, even if we don't exactly want it. It's sometimes about creating needs and sometimes about amplifying those that we already have.

Father Kotler says that marketing is about improving life, even if just a little. It's about connecting people who have an unsolved problem with a solution. At its best, it changes the way people consume and enhances the quality of life. At its worst, it manipulates and exploits our innermost desires and fears for profit.

But if we are honest with ourselves, it's an honest form of human expression. It doesn't hide us from our flaws. It takes them, solves them, pokes fun at them and sometimes makes money through them.

But, the more we think about it, the less sense it makes.

Marketing is simple. It's behavior change at scale.

It's about a change in mindsets and habits and pushing people towards embracing new outward identities. It's about understanding people so well, that you're able to nudge their choices in a certain way. And sometimes that's for good - like nudging them away from fried to baked chips.

We shouldn't feel that marketing is only about manipulation. It's about translation. Great research and intimacy with consumers help us translate their hidden desires, fears and eccentricities into something of value. It's an endless experiment in psychology and a pretty exciting one at that. And those of us who get to see it up close, we should consider ourselves lucky. As I do.

It Never Ends

If you've made it this far into the book then, first of all, congratulations. Secondly, you're now a part of the tribe. You're among the select few among the billions of humans who understand the hidden language of nudges, tricks and stories.

It's a world that's as exciting as it's bewildering at times. But there's never a boring day.

Unlike the hard sciences, any rabbit hole into the psychology of marketing can never end. The answers are never conclusive and the questions always keep on changing. I think Marketing is a philosophy at the end of the day and like most good philosophies, it raises more questions than it answers.

And with that, I leave you with this:

It's never only about the *buy*, it's about the *why*.

Thank you for diving into the depths of our mind with me. Now, if you've felt a nudge to recommend this book to someone else, that's just marketing. Again.

ABOUT THE AUTHOR

Harinder Singh Pelia is a man with three great obsessions: marketing, memes, and mutton biryani - in no particular order (*though let's be honest, biryani would win*). Since the age of 18, he's been hooked on marketing, either studying it, doing it, or persuading someone else to fall for it. He's led marketing teams at Amazon, Ajio Luxe, Diesel, and other brands that you've probably spent too much money on.

Currently pursuing a PhD in marketing at XLRI Jamshedpur, he's also the founder of the 10Xer Club, a community for India's best marketers to upskill, network, land jobs, and occasionally rant over a beer or two. And yes, he's got a podcast too, because, well, everyone does now.

www.ingramcontent.com/pod-product-compliance
Lightning Source LLC
Chambersburg PA
CBHW021530150726
47990CB00006B/2168